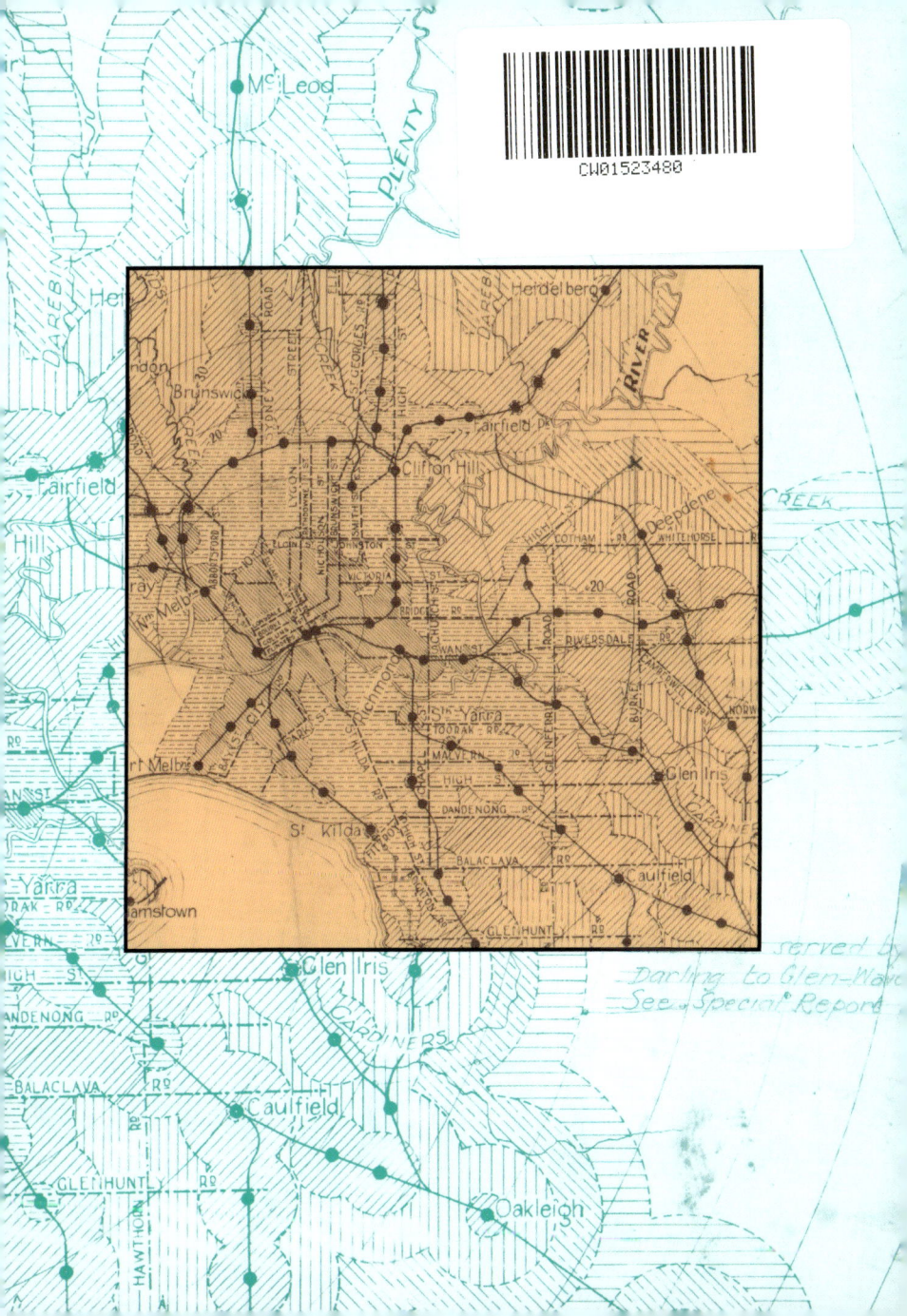

served by
Darling to Glen-Wave
See Special Report

— MAP OF —

— MELBOURNE AND SUBURBS —

MELBOURNE
COCKTAILS

AN ELEGANT COLLECTION OF OVER 100 RECIPES INSPIRED BY AUSTRALIA'S NIGHTLIFE CAPITAL

ALANA HOUSE

CIDER MILL PRESS

BOOK PUBLISHERS

MELBOURNE COCKTAILS

ISBN-13: 978-1-40034-892-3
ISBN-10: 1-40034-892-7

This book may be ordered by mail from the publisher. Please include $5.99 for postage and handling. Please support your local bookseller first!

Books published by Cider Mill Press Book Publishers are available at special discounts for bulk purchases in the United States by corporations, institutions, and other organizations. For more information, please contact the publisher.

Cider Mill Press Book Publishers
"Where good books are ready for press"
501 Nelson Place
Nashville, Tennessee 37214
cidermillpress.com

Typography: Copperplate, Headline Gothic, SodaScript, Sackers, Warnock

Photography credits on page 279

Printed in India

24 25 26 27 28 REP 5 4 3 2 1

First Edition

CONTENTS

INTRODUCTION

Drinking History Tours in action

If you are seeking the nightlife capital of Australia, you will find it in Melbourne. When the sun sets, the city lights up with live music and vibrant drinks at thousands of bars, pubs, and clubs. On history-filled corners, down atmospheric laneways, and on scenic rooftops you will find some of the world's best bartenders shaking innovative cocktails until the sun rises again.

According to Drinking History Tours founder Ben Oliver, booze has played a key role in the city's history from the moment it was founded. Only settled by Europeans in 1835, Melbourne wasted no time in establishing its nighttime economy. By 1839 the town boasted twenty pubs. "I always knew Melbourne had a great bar scene," Oliver says, "[but] what I didn't realize was the weird confluence of historical factors that came together like a jigsaw puzzle to build the city in the first place. Our first mayor was a brewer, the first meeting of the Melbourne City Council took place inside a pub, and, five years after Melbourne was founded, there was one pub for every two hundred and forty people."

Cocktails were not on the menu in those early days. The pubs served shots of rum, with beer slowly gaining in popularity over the decades that followed.

Brews were weak and often infused with tobacco to make them appear stronger. They were colloquially known as "swipes" because patrons had to drink them down in one gulp to avoid the terrible taste.

Melbourne, 1869

Flinders Lane, circa 1860

THE GOLD RUSH AND THE SIX O'CLOCK SWILL

When gold was discovered near Melbourne in the early 1850s, the city's population exploded from 23,000 to 150,000 in less than seven years. A proliferation of pubs followed, including the Duke of Wellington, located on the corner of Flinders and Russell Streets in the city. Established in 1853, you can still order a round of drinks at its atmospheric front bar.

During the 1850s the heaviest traffic in Australia was on the roads connecting Melbourne to Bendigo, a town eighty-two miles to the northwest of the city. Bendigo produced the most gold in the world from 1850 to 1900 and the thoroughfares leading to the town were lined with the colonial equivalent of pop-up bars—canvas tents serving rum to thirsty travelers.

By the 1880s the vast wealth pouring into the city led it to be christened "Marvellous Melbourne," and it had a reputation for being one of the world's biggest and most cosmopolitan cities.

However, strict licensing laws during the First World War dealt a crippling blow to its sophistication. The government introduced a six o'clock closing time at hotels and pubs as an austerity measure and an attempt to improve public morality.

The ruling was quickly nicknamed "the six o'clock swill," as it sparked a last-minute rush among workers to buy as many drinks as possible before hotels closed. Pubs catered to the frenzy by building longer bars, employing more staff, and tiling the walls and floors for ease of post-closing cleaning.

Swanston Street

In 1956, journalist Reg Leonard bemoaned in the city's *Sun News-Pictorial* newspaper: "In the past year I have travelled thousands of miles through the United States, Britain, the Continent, and Mediterranean. I will say at once that nowhere have I experienced anything as revolting and disgusting as what we call the six o'clock swill. The daily demonstration of piggery is something no other country in the world can match."

Melbourne hosted the Olympic Games in the same year, with a *New York Times* correspondent sardonically reporting: "The six o'clock swill is a charming folk custom which requires saloons to stop serving liquor at 6 p.m. This creates a challenge which no Aussie worth his malt will take lying down, or at least not as long as he can stand."

The six o'clock swill lasted fifty years in the city, finally ending in Melbourne in 1966, but the era was not entirely without refinement.

In 1935 the city welcomed one of Australia's first small bars, Jimmy Watson's. Located in the inner-city suburb of Carlton, the bar championed wine at a time when it was far from fashionable. "Three-penny dark" port and sweet sherry were the most consumed wine products, but owner Jim Watson was determined to change that. Around 1940 he started purchasing wines from vineyards and educating his customers on his favorite wine styles: dry whites, young reds, and great fortified wines.

To this day, the bar remains family owned, maintains its traditional charm, and still holds bottles of fortified wine from as early as 1919 in its cellar, with a selection of spritzes and spirits joining wine on the menu in recent decades.

MELBOURNE'S LANEWAY CULTURE IS BORN

However, it wasn't until the 1980s that Melbourne's modern cocktail scene really began to flourish, producing one of the disco era's favorite drinks, the Japanese Slipper.

A young French bartender called Jean-Paul Bourguignon was working at Mietta's Restaurant when he was handed a bottle of a new spirit called Midori by a sales representative. He decided to mix the melon liqueur with Cointreau and fresh lemon juice, and a mixology legend was born.

According to Punch, the drink's simple build and fresh citrus have earned it a place alongside New York's Cosmopolitan and London's Bramble as Melbourne's contribution to the early days of the cocktail revival.

The Keys Leisure Centre

A decade later the city welcomed a small bar revolution when Crown Casino opened on the banks of Melbourne's Yarra River. A new form of liquor licence was introduced by the government to allow the casino to operate bars without needing to serve food. Removing the requirement to have kitchens led to more than 152 small bar applications being lodged between 1994 and 1997 alone.

"This simple change transformed the economics for bars," says Ben Oliver, who takes locals and visitors on walking tours that combine visits to some of the city's best bars with local lore and stories. "The new licences, combined with cheap inner-city rents at the time, largely led to our laneway bar culture."

MELBOURNE'S PRODIGAL SON: SAM ROSS

Melbourne can also take credit for producing one of the world's most famous bartenders, Sam Ross.

Sam, who spent many years behind the bar at New York's iconic Milk & Honey and was named 2011 American Bartender of the Year, is famed for creating modern cocktail classics including the Penicillin and the Paper Plane.

His career kicked off as a teenager, while helping his mother and sister open a bar called Ginger on Brunswick Street, Fitzroy. Within a few years, Brunswick Street had gained the reputation of being the

epicenter of the Australian cocktail scene, with bars including the famed Black Pearl opening nearby.

When the bright lights of New York City beckoned, Sam convinced the founder of Milk & Honey, Sasha Petraske, to hire him. A year later, Sam created the Penicillin, a cocktail that expertly blended Scotch whisky with fresh lemon juice and honey-ginger syrup, finished with a barspoon of smoky Islay whisky floated on top.

As Australia's *Gourmet Traveller* magazine notes, the Penicillin has attracted a cult following "akin to that of Dick Bradsell's Bramble or Dale DeGroff's Whiskey Smash" and appears on cocktail lists in establishments all over the world.

Beverly Rooftop

MODERN MELBOURNE

Melbourne bartenders have continued to make their mark globally over the years, including Orlando Marzo from the boundary-pushing Lume restaurant in South Melbourne, who bested more than ten thousand bartenders to win the 2018 Diageo World Class competition. And now, in the 2020s, Melbourne's bar scene is the equal to any major city in the world.

In 2024, bartending legend Dale DeGroff launched the inaugural cocktail list for Grey Goose's first-ever standalone bar, Le Martini, in the city. "The city has no shortage of excellent drinking establishments, so it was meant to be," says DeGroff. As for how the city's bar scene differentiates from Sydney, DeGroff describes Melbourne as having a more neighbourhood feel.

Former Diageo World Class Australian Bartender of the Year Nick Tesar, who is creative director of drinks at Australian craft gin distillery Four Pillars, believes the "beautiful hospitality" of the city and its access to incredible produce are what makes the Melbourne bar scene so memorable.

Lui Bar

The city, which is the capital of the state of Victoria, is home to more than one hundred and twenty distilleries, more than six hundred and ninety-nine wineries, and more than one hundred and fifty craft breweries, giving bartenders access to an unprecedented selection of locally produced products.

"Currently, smaller, more personality-driven bars are doing well," Tesar says. "Venues that also focus on more than just drinks, that can tell their own story and have a genuine connection with their customers, are thriving."

Moon Dog Brewing "flavourologist" Chris Hysted-Adams, who helmed Melbourne's Black Pearl when it won Best International Cocktail bar at the 2017 Spirited Awards, agrees that quality is king in the city. "Apart from having access to unique ingredients that are available nowhere else in the world, we have an amazing culinary community that we work closely with day to day," he says. "We're also frighteningly creative—the laid back but 'can-do' nature of Australians can lead to some unique results."

HOW TO DRINK LIKE A MELBURNIAN

To truly experience Melbourne's cocktail culture, it's important to know how to drink like a local.

Start by exploring the city's historic arcades and art-filled laneways. It's the perfect way to both experience Melbourne and enjoy its thriving bar scene.

Then admire the city skyline from its remarkable array of rooftop bars and terraces, which have proliferated since smoking was banned in venues in 2007.

Trinket

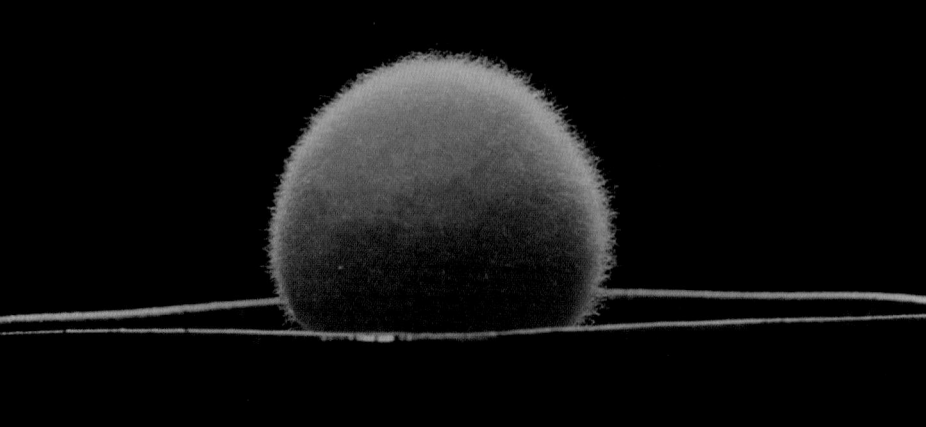

Bad Apple

While Melbourne is Australia's coffee capital—its residents love to sip lattes by day and Espresso Martinis by night—Melburnians also love to try new things.

A boundary-pushing cocktail called Bad Apple, for example, won the title of Drink of the Year at the Boothby 2023 Drink of the Year Awards. Created by bartender Samuel Thornhill at BYRDI, it featured apple brandy and oloroso sherry and was served with a fermented apple as its garnish. Those who ordered it were instructed to eat the furry apple first and then drink the cocktail.

Melbourne bartenders love to experiment with native ingredients too, such as saltbush, Davidson plum, and lemon myrtle, mixed with local craft spirits to create concoctions that are truly unique.

It's also important to know the local drinking customs. For example, it is common to buy rounds of drinks for your friends, which are called "shouts."

Shouts invariably go hand in hand with sporting events, as Melburnians love their sport and cocktails in equal measure. The city is home to a calendar of major events that bring the city to a literal standstill and fill its bars with patrons.

A public holiday is held on the first Tuesday in November for the Melbourne Cup. Known as the "race that stops the nation," more than a million viewers watch the event, many with a glass of champagne or cocktail in hand.

More than eighty thousand people flock to Flemington Racecourse to be trackside for the race, and its famed "The Birdcage" enclosure fills with celebrities, influencers, and Victorian Racing Club members and their guests. Drinks brands spend hundreds of thousands of dollars building extravagant marquees to entertain guests and toast the race.

Melburnians also celebrate an AFL Grand Final Eve Public Holiday. AFL stands for the Australian Football League, the national body for Australian Rules Football, a game that was born in Victoria in 1858 to keep cricket players fit during the off-season.

Melbourne remains the game's heartland, and it has become a sport that transcends age, demographic, and gender. It is watched by more than eight million Australians each year at live matches, on television, and in pubs and clubs around the nation.

Other hugely popular sporting events are the Australian Open tennis tournament in January and the Australian Grand Prix in March. While neither event can claim its own public holiday, both bring a carnival atmosphere to the city.

Morris House

The stands and numerous pop-up bars at Albert Park are packed with more than 450,000 fans from across Victoria, interstate, and overseas each year during the Formula 1 Australian Grand Prix. The event also turbocharges Melbourne nightlife, with many bars hosting special Grand Prix nights and creating signature cocktails to celebrate the race.

SETTING UP A MELBOURNE HOME BAR

BY SCOTT ALLAN

If you want to bring the flavors of Melbourne's cocktail culture into your own home, it's important to know how to set up and stock your bar.

While you can repurpose to-go coffee cups or plastic containers as cocktail shakers and open corked bottles by inserting the base into a shoe and knocking it into a wall, there is no denying that having the right tools for the job makes the process easier and more satisfying. By arranging a small station at home that can be exclusively used for making drinks, you'll find yourself enjoying both the process and the result. In the world of bartending, much like the world of cooking, your workstation is your own zone, and when it is in order, you set yourself up for success.

Two things you need to access quickly when mixing drinks are running water and ice. If you choose a spot close to these two things, almost everything else can be easily brought to your station. No bartender worth their saline solution leaves dirty equipment lying around, particularly when a quick rinse with hot water will render almost any piece of kit ready to go for the next cocktail.

Ice is the most fiddly part when it comes to making drinks at home. Often the number of cocktails you can make will be limited by the amount of ice you have ready to go. Professionals have the luxury of incredible ice-making machines that churn out perfectly clear cubes, together with deep stainless steel wells to store them, dedicated freezers for clear blocks, plus spheres and spears for those important final touches. Fridges with ice dispensers are magic for solving the first part of this problem at home; otherwise you'll be stockpiling ice ahead of a party.

That's the basics covered, now let's get to the fun stuff. This is the equipment you need to get started:

- Dedicated large chopping board with juice groove (no onion or garlic from dinner prep in your drinks, please!)
- 2 sets of Boston/cocktail shakers
- 1 mixing glass
- 1 multilevel jigger
- 1 barspoon
- 1 paring knife (or other sharp, compact knife)
- 1 Hawthorne strainer
- 1 conical fine-mesh strainer
- Good quality waiter's friend (with a hinged corkscrew and a sharp knife)

And for those who want to get fancy:

- 1 julep strainer
- Cocktail picks
- Bitters dasher bottles
- Muddler
- Atomiser
- Squeezy bottles for syrups
- Tabletop ice bucket and ice scoop
- Sharp peeler

There are lots of great videos online showing how to use everything listed above, plus an endless list of recipes to try. Along the way, try my favorite whiskey cocktail, a Sazerac!

SIMPLE SYRUP: In a small saucepan over medium-low heat, combine 1 cup water and 1 cup sugar and stir, simmering, until the sugar is dissolved. Allow the syrup to cool.

YOUR SPIRITS STARTER KIT

When looking to stock your shelves with ingredients, I'd recommend starting with those needed to make classic cocktails that only require a few ingredients—Martini, Manhattan, Old Fashioned, Negroni—and then branching out from there.

- Ideally buy items that are likely to get a lot of use. If a recipe calls for a small amount of something obscure and you don't love that drink, you might just end up with a space in your cupboard dedicated to that one cocktail for a long time.
- Start with good-quality spirits, but not top of the line. If you find you really like a particular cocktail, then try stepping up an ingredient and seeing if you like how the drink changes.
- Also be aware that some ingredients such as vermouths or other low-ABV wine-based products should really be stored in the refrigerator.

It's been interesting to see whiskey evolve as a cocktail ingredient in Melbourne over the past decade. Not that long ago, whiskey was seen as too complex and too strongly flavored to play nicely with others in cocktails, and many thought trying to do so was ruining the sacred character of the spirit. Thanks to innovative Melbourne bartenders, we now balance, infuse, adjust, and create mind-blowing flavor bombs with every kind of spirit.

I recommend stocking whiskey with a slightly higher ABV than usual for cocktails. Most easily accessible products are around 40% ABV, and at this proof (80 proof), once you add other ingredients, sugar, and dilution, their flavor is significantly reduced. You can regularly find American whiskeys at 45% and Scotch or Australian whiskies at 46%, and I rarely prefer making drinks with products under this level. Cask-strength whiskies can taste incredible in cocktails, but never underestimate their ability to cut your night short.

TOP TIPS FOR ENSURING PERFECT SERVES AT HOME

1. Find glassware you love to use. It's a big part of the pleasure of consuming cocktails. You can revel in the way the glass feels in your fingertips and on your lips, the way it makes your drink look (in person or online), and even the sound it makes when you clink it with another in a cheers with a friend.

2. Have great mixers on hand. I always keep tonic, which I love with amaro, and soda for my Whiskey Highballs on hand in single-serve bottles, with at least one of each in the fridge. That ensures every serve is perfectly fresh and you're never throwing away a mixer that's gone flat.

3. Seek out low-sugar mixers and cocktail ingredients that aren't artificially sweetened—they are great for letting the flavor of your chosen spirit shine and not putting you through glucose withdrawals the morning after.

4. Taste for balance. The best skill you can develop when making cocktails at home is to taste as you go and balance your drinks before you serve them. Bartenders all have their own thoughts on the ratios of ingredients in classic recipes, but all are trying to achieve a harmonious collection of flavors and sensations. If you taste your drink and it is too sweet, you can correct that before it goes into the glass by adding a touch of another ingredient or giving it a little extra dilution in the shaker or mixing glass. Once you can identify what a drink might need to make it a little more perfect, you can be confident in trying any recipe or even making up your own.

Scott Allan is the on-premises and events expert at The Whisky List, Australia's largest online whiskey store.

MELBOURNE COCKTAILS

MARCO POLO

BIANCHETTO
26-28 COTHAM ROAD, KEW

The Marco Polo was inspired by the famed explorer and his travels. Bartender Marco Pellegrini says the drink echoes his spirit of adventure by combining ingredients from Italy, Asia, and Australia. The cocktail's star ingredient is lemon myrtle–infused gin. Lemon myrtle is a popular flavor in Australian mixology—the aromatic native shrub gives the spirit a crisp citrus taste that combines perfectly with the other the ingredients in the drink, providing balance and zing. If lemon myrtle–infused gin is not available, choose any gin with lemon accents. Gazzosa is a sparkling soft drink from Italy, which is also home to Contratto Aperitif. Similar to Aperol, Contratto is made by one of Italy's oldest sparkling wine producers.

GLASSWARE: Highball glass

GARNISH: Orange twist

- ⅔ oz. | 20 ml lemon myrtle–infused gin
- 1½ oz. | 45 ml yuzu liqueur
- 1 oz. | 30 ml Contratto Aperitif
- Dash grapefruit bitters
- Gazzosa Cortese, to top

1. Combine all of the ingredients, except for the Gazzosa, in a highball glass.
2. Slowly pour in the Gazzosa. Lightly stir the ingredients.
3. Add ice cubes one at a time.
4. Express an orange peel over the drink and garnish with a fresh orange twist.

SPICY WATERMELON MARGARITA

MORRIS HOUSE
120 EXHIBITION STREET

Venue manager Dylan Hewlett says the beauty of Morris House is that it combines all the best bits of Melbourne in one location. "We have an awesome rooftop, a basement comedy club, delicious food, and a great selection of cocktails for any occasion," he says. "It's the one-stop-shop for a great day or night out in the CBD." A Spicy Margarita is a go-to cocktail in Melbourne and Hewlett says he loves that no matter where you try one, it will always taste slightly different. "You could get lost in the city just tasting them all," he says.

GLASSWARE: Coupe glass

GARNISH: Chile oil

- Tajín, for the rim
- 1 oz. | 30 ml Olmeca Altos Plata
- ½ oz. | 15 ml Cointreau
- ½ oz. | 15 ml agave nectar
- 1 oz. | 30 ml watermelon syrup
- 1 oz. | 30 ml fresh lime juice
- 2 dashes Tabasco Green Jalapeño Pepper Sauce

1. Dip the side of a coupe glass in water then dip the glass in Tajín.
2. Combine the remaining ingredients in a Boston shaker, add ice, and shake well until the shaker ices over.
3. Double-strain the cocktail into the rimmed coupe and garnish with chile oil.

HAVANA NIGHTS

The Ghost of Alfred Felton is located inside one of Melbourne's most iconic pubs, The Esplanade, affectionately known among locals as "The Espy." The grand seaside hotel has been a centerpiece of the suburb of St Kilda since 1878. "Using a whipped cream gun really helps to give the drink another dimension, not only in flavor—but also texture," operations and systems manager Ryan Dobbie says. "It creates a melted marshmallow/meringue feeling that lingers on your lips." If you don't have access the specific liqueur used here, use any macadamia liqueur.

GLASSWARE: Rocks glass

GARNISH: Fresh nutmeg, blue orchid flower

- 1 oz. | 30 ml Coconut Fat–Washed Rum (see recipe on page 39)
- 1 oz. | 30 ml Mac. Liqueur by Brookie's
- ⅔ oz. | 20 ml fresh lemon juice
- ⅓ oz. | 10 ml simple syrup
- Passion Fruit Foam (see recipe on page 39), to top

1. Combine all of the ingredients, except for the foam, in a Boston shaker with ice and shake hard until the tins form some ice crystallisation on the outside.

2. Place a large ice cube into a rocks glass and double-strain the cocktail into the glass.

3. Grab the Passion Fruit Foam whipped cream gun, release the canister, and give it another good shake.

4. Holding the cream gun upside down, pull the trigger gently and create a smooth layer of foam on top of the drink, right up to the top of the glass.

5. Grab some nutmeg and a grater and create a fine dusting on the top of the foam.

6. Garnish with a blue orchid flower.

COCONUT FAT–WASHED RUM: In a saucepan over low heat, add 100 grams coconut oil and warm it until it becomes liquid. Remove from heat and allow the coconut oil to cool slightly, then pour it into a large (34 oz. [1 liter]) jar. Pour most of a bottle—22 oz. (700 ml)—of dark rum into the jar, put the lid on the jar, and give it a hard shake. Leave the mixture at room temperature for 4 to 5 hours for the flavors to infuse, then put the jar in the freezer overnight for the fat to solidify on top. Using a knife, make a hole through the solidified fat. Pour the rum through a fine-mesh strainer. If necessary, fine-strain again to remove any leftover solids.

PASSION FRUIT FOAM: This recipe will give you quite a lot of foam. If you are planning on making only a couple of drinks, you can cut the volumes in halves or quarters. Begin by making Honey Water: in a small container, combine 3⅓ oz. (100 ml) hot water and 1 to 2 teaspoons honey and stir. Place 8½ (250 ml) egg whites, 3⅓ oz. (100 ml) simple syrup, 3⅓ oz. (100 ml) passion fruit puree, and 1¾ oz. (50 ml) of the Honey Water into a whipped cream gun and give it a good shake. Set the cream gun aside for later use.

PRIMA BALLERINA

Regulars love Trinket for its old-school charm and the array of eponymous trinkets that decorate the venue. The bar also has a secret little spot downstairs that is found only when patrons venture through a wardrobe door. The finishing touch for the Prima Ballerina is a raspberry dust rim, created using freeze-dried raspberries that are ground into a powder, which intensifies the flavor of the fruit.

GLASSWARE: Coupe glass

- **Raspberry dust, for the rim**
- **2 oz. | 60 ml gin**
- **1 oz. | 30 ml cranberry juice**
- **½ oz. | 15 ml fresh lemon juice**
- **⅔ oz. | 20 ml Pineapple Shrub (see recipe)**
- **Dash rhubarb bitters**

1. Wet the rim of a coupe then dip the glass rim into the raspberry dust.
2. Combine the remaining ingredients in a Boston shaker with ice and shake.
3. Double-strain the cocktail into the rimmed coupe.

PINEAPPLE SHRUB: Combine 34 oz. (1 liter) fresh pineapple juice, 1¼ pounds (600 grams) white sugar, and 5 oz. (150 ml) apple cider vinegar. Mix until combined and the shrub is ready to serve.

CHERUB

State of Grace venue manager Chelsea Allan says the Cherub is the perfect cocktail to cap off the night. "It has Melbourne written all over it," she explains. "Cherub is a sweet cocktail, which makes it perfect for dessert." A good hard shake is vital to ensure the sorbet is well incorporated into the drink. Allan also suggests using a whipped cream cannister to create the foam, as it will give the cocktail a heavenly creamy texture from the first sip to the last.

GLASSWARE: Martini glass

- 1½ oz. | 45 ml vodka
- ½ oz. | 15 ml Chambord
- ½ oz. | 15 ml macadamia liqueur
- ½ oz. | 15 ml fresh lemon juice
- ⅓ oz. | 10 ml raspberry sorbet
- White Chocolate Espuma (see recipe), to top

1. Combine all of the ingredients, except for the white chocolate, in a cocktail shaker with ice and shake.

2. Double-strain the cocktail into a martini glass.

3. Top with White Chocolate Espuma: holding the cream gun upside down, pull the trigger gently and create a smooth layer of foam on top of the drink, right up to the top of the glass.

WHITE CHOCOLATE ESPUMA: Combine 10 oz. (300 ml) white crème de cacao and 10 oz. (300 ml) simple syrup with 1 egg white in a whipped cream cannister.

HAYDEN SCOTT LAMBERT, ABOVE BOARD

Above Board is one of Melbourne's most globally renowned bars and has appeared on The World's 50 Best Bars list. The bar, which has only sixteen seats, is warm and minimal, with an intimate charm that owner and head bartender Hayden Scott Lambert says "draws you in."

There is no backbar or any visible bottles on display, as Hayden prefers patrons to focus on flavor rather than brand names. "We provide the utmost service, a smashing cocktail list, and our staff are friendly and welcoming," he says. "I think customers enjoy our style of service along with the unique design of the bar and, above all, the wonderful hospitality they receive."

H.S.L SPECIAL

The H.S.L Special is the cornerstone of Above Board's cocktail list and gets its name from owner and head bartender Hayden Scott Lambert's initials. "It is a complex cocktail that has great balance," he says. "Aesthetically it looks sharp and delicious due to its deep red color . . . very Instagrammable! But most importantly, it tastes absolutely amazing." The cocktail's hero ingredient is Amaro Montenegro, which Hayden describes as "the most delicious Amaro out there." Substitute any blackberry liqueur for the Marionette Mûre.

GLASSWARE: Small sour glass

GARNISH: Blackberry dusted in powdered sugar

- 1¼ oz. | 35 ml Amaro Montenegro
- 17/20 oz. | 25 ml fresh lime juice
- ½ oz. | 15 ml Marionette Mûre
- ¼ oz. | 7.5 ml 2:1 Simple Syrup (see recipe)
- Dash Pernod Absinthe

1. Combine all of the ingredients in a cocktail shaker with ice and shake.
2. Strain the cocktail into a small sour glass over cracked ice.
3. Garnish with a blackberry dusted in powdered sugar.

2:1 SIMPLE SYRUP: In a small saucepan over medium-low heat, combine 2 cups sugar and 1 cup water and heat, stirring until the sugar is dissolved. Allow the syrup to cool.

JAPANESE SLIPPER

ABOVE BOARD
1/306 SMITH STREET, COLLINGWOOD

The iconic Japanese Slipper cocktail was created in Melbourne in 1984 by Frenchman Jean-Paul Bourguignon while he was working at a bar called Mietta's. Decades later, the cocktail is undergoing a revival and features on drinks menus at many bars throughout the city, including Above Board. Above Board owner and head bartender Hayden Scott Lambert has created his own take on the original, adding ingredients including lime juice and orange bitters.

GLASSWARE: Coupe glass

- 1¼ oz. | 35 ml Midori
- ⅔ oz. | 20 ml fresh lemon juice
- ½ oz. | 15 ml orange curaçao
- ¼ oz. | 7.5 ml fresh lime juice
- Dash orange bitters
- Dash Malic Acid Solution (see recipe)

1. Combine all of the ingredients in a cocktail shaker with ice and shake.

2. Fine-strain the cocktail into a coupe and serve up.

MALIC ACID SOLUTION: Combine 10 grams malic acid powder with 100 grams (100 ml) water. Whisk to dissolve the powder, then bottle the solution.

SNEAKY LINK

The Sneaky Link was a finalist in the rhubarb aperitif brand RHUBI Mistelle's cocktail challenge, which celebrated the versatility and ease of switching out key ingredients for RHUBI Mistelle in cocktails. Crafted in Victoria from fresh Aussie rhubarb, RHUBI Mistelle is made by pairing fermented rhubarb juice with juniper spirit, gentian, grapefruit, and mandarin skins. Above Board bartender Paige Chambert took the top spot in Victoria with her perfectly balanced cocktail.

GLASSWARE: Coupe glass

- 17/20 oz. | 25 ml Tanqueray London Dry Gin
- 17/20 oz. | 25 ml Mancino Vermouth di Torino Bianco Ambrato
- ⅔ oz. | 20 ml fresh lemon juice
- 1 teaspoon | 5 ml RHUBI Mistelle
- 1 teaspoon | 5 ml Campari
- Dash orange bitters

1. Combine all of the ingredients in a cocktail shaker with ice and shake.
2. Double-strain the cocktail into a coupe.

OATHKEEPER

MOLLY ROSE
279-285 WELLINGTON STREET, COLLINGWOOD

From the moment small neighborhood brewery and bar Molly Rose opened in Collingwood in 2019, it has aimed to break the stereotypical perception of what a traditional brewery bar should be. At the heart of the venue is a stunning centerpiece bar that features limited-release and core-range beers, a concise and mostly Australian wine list, and a craft cocktail list. Behind the bar are Wayan Geard and Ryan Cassidy, who say the secret to the popular Oathkeeper is the addition of centennial hops, which gives the drink a "pep that people aren't expecting," says Geard. "Craft beer enthusiasts often appreciate the complexity and distinctiveness that hops can bring to a beverage. It's a nod to Melbourne's renowned craft beer scene, all encapsulated in a single drink experience."

GLASSWARE: Coupe glass

- 1 oz. | 30 ml Fat-Washed Bay Leaf Olive Oil Vodka (see recipe)
- 1 oz. | 30 ml gin
- 1 teaspoon | 5 ml Cocchi Americano
- 1 teaspoon | 5 ml Dolin Dry Vermouth
- 2 dashes orange bitters
- 3 sprays Centennial Hop Tincture (see recipe)

1. Combine all of the ingredients in a mixing glass with ice and stir the cocktail down.
2. Strain the cocktail into a coupe glass.

FAT-WASHED BAY LEAF OLIVE OIL VODKA: Begin by making bay leaf–infused olive oil: Combine fresh bay leaves and olive oil in a 30:70 mixture. Then sous vide the infusion on low heat. Strain the leaves out once the color of the oil has become darker, slightly greener, and the oil tastes herbal. Finish by fat-washing the vodka. Combine 3½ oz. (100 ml) bay leaf–infused olive oil with 2 cups (500 ml) vodka and shake vigorously. Sous vide the mixture for 1 hour. Let the mixture infuse at least overnight after the initial heating. Place the vodka in the freezer until the oil is solid. The oil should freeze, leaving only the alcohol behind. Strain the vodka.

CENTENNIAL HOP TINCTURE: Place 40 grams macerated hops in 6¾ oz. (200 ml) 60% alcohol spirits under a CO_2 blanket. Filter out the hops and let the tincture settle for 24 hours. Keep the tincture in a spray bottle.

AMERICANO

Lumen People owner Marichi Clarke says the humble Americano, when executed with quality elements, is one of his all-time favorite cocktails because it is equally versatile at the beginning of an evening or beautifully bookending a night out. "This rendition comes to us via our wine importing pal, Liz Carey from Vivant Selections, who brings the crucial element of Partida Creus MUZ Natural Vermouth to the cocktail. She also, to our absolute pleasure, passed along this original recipe by her pal Nick Tesar from his time at Bar Liberty," Marichi explains. "It's spritzy enough to keep it lighthearted, but layered enough to keep you interested all the way through. 'Moreish' is the best way we can describe it. Our guests often ask us what's in it, which is always a great sign you've hit the mark."

GLASSWARE: Medium-tall glass

GARNISH: Orange slice

- 1 oz. | 30 ml Partida Creus MUZ Natural Vermouth

- 1 oz. | 30 ml Marionette Bitter Curaçao

- 3 oz. | 90 ml Strangelove Very Mandarin Lo-Cal Soda

1. Add all of the ingredients, in the order listed, to a medium-tall glass with a block of ice.
2. Stir gently and garnish with an orange slice.

PAAWAN ENGINEER, MILL PLACE MERCHANTS

Mill Place Merchants is tucked away at the end of Mill Place off Flinders Lane inside a heritage-listed nineteenth-century building. Once home to the Flemington Meat Preserving Company, the building has been lovingly revived, showcasing its original bluestone walls and exposed wooden beams. Guests enter through a monogrammed red door and find themselves in an old dressing room filled with mannequins, rolls of fabric, and a vintage sewing machine. The decor is a nod to the many garment workers who once called the former rag-trade district home.

A grand gilt-framed mirror provides a secret entrance to the bar that lies beyond, a cozy, opulent room adorned with Victorian wingback chairs, chaise lounges, and leather chesterfields. At the heart of Mill Place Merchants stands a gleaming copper-topped bar, where expertly crafted original cocktails are served against a backdrop of vintage bottles, glasses, and silver trays. The bar team is led by Paawan Engineer, who has created a welcoming space, not only for himself but for all Melburnians and visitors to the city to enjoy.

"When guests step through the door, they are treated like old friends returning to their favorite venue," he says. "It's not just about the drinks or the ambience; it's about the people, the relationships, creating lasting memories and fostering a sense of community for everyone who walks through our doors."

The drinks menu has been designed by award-winning Italian mixologist Giancarlo Mancino. Paying homage to the cocktail masters of old, the menu acknowledges Jacques Straub, author of *Straub's Manual of Mixed Drinks*, Dick Bradsell, creator of the Espresso Martini, and Hyman Gale & Gerald F. Marco, authors of *The How and When* cocktail book, which was first printed in 1938.

LA LOUISIANE

La Louisiane is a stirred rye whiskey libation, which was the house cocktail at La Louisiane, a New Orleans institution famous for its fiery Cajun specialties. Originally appearing in Stanley Clisby Arthur's *Famous New Orleans Drinks and How to Mix 'Em* in 1937, this lost New Orleans classic was recently adapted and featured in Jim Meehan's *The PDT Cocktail Book*. Bar manager Paawan Engineer explains that both Melbourne and New Orleans were built on the banks of a river and, although not as influential a jazz capital as New Orleans, Melburnians have very good taste in jazz and enjoy their cocktails passionately.

GLASSWARE: Coupe glass

GARNISH: Maraschino cherry, orange peel

- 1⅓ oz. | 40 ml rye whiskey
- ⅔ oz. | 20 ml rosso vermouth
- ⅓ oz. | 10 ml Bénédictine
- Dash absinthe
- Dash Peychaud's bitters

1. Chill a coupe glass in the freezer. Combine all of the ingredients in a mixing glass.
2. Add some good quality ice and stir until the mixing glass starts to frost.
3. Strain the cocktail into the chilled coupe glass.
4. To garnish, twist an orange peel over the drink and offer a maraschino cherry on the side or in the drink (skewered).

VELUDA

Pincho Disco matches Latin American food with cocktails. Head bartender Jordan Alber says the fusion of an elevated dining experience with an energetic and raucous bar creates an atmosphere that encourages customers to make a night of it. The Veluda, a Milk Punch cocktail, is the preferred after-shift sipper for the bar staff, leading them to recommend it to all their favorite guests. "It drinks smooth and silky with the prickle of chile—hence the name in Portuguese, meaning 'velvet,'" Alber says.

GLASSWARE: Rocks glass

GARNISH: Orange twist

- 1 oz. | 30 ml Chile-Infused Patrón Silver (see recipe)
- 1 oz. | 30 ml Tempranillo
- ⅔ oz. | 20 ml fresh lemon juice
- ½ oz. | 15 ml apricot brandy
- ½ oz. | 15 ml blackberry syrup
- ⅔ oz. | 20 ml milk

1. Combine all of the ingredients, except for the milk, in a container and stir.
2. Pour the mixture into the milk and allow the milk to curdle for 1 hour before straining through a coffee filter. The liquid will take time to start coming through clear.
3. Refilter the cloudy liquid.
4. In a rocks glass, stir the liquid down with ice to chill and dilute it before serving with an orange twist.

CHILE-INFUSED PATRÓN SILVER: Add 2 birds-eye chile peppers, chopped, to 1 (750 ml) bottle of Patrón Silver Tequila. Let the mixture infuse for at least for 24 hours then strain and rebottle.

MATT AMBLER, ROSSI BAR

Since opening in 2023, Rossi has attracted regulars who return for the relaxed atmosphere and modern Italian bites. The venue offers an irresistible trifecta of Italian dining, late-night cocktails, and carefully curated music in the heart of the inner-Melbourne suburb of Prahran.

Beverage manager Matt Ambler says Rossi seamlessly blends delicious food with great service in a moody and trendy setting. "A strong focus is placed on the aesthetic and the feel of the place, with DJs playing upbeat house music most nights of the week," he explains.

D'ORO FIZZ

ROSSI BAR
162 GREVILLE STREET, PRAHRAN

Beverage manager Matt Ambler says the D'oro Fizz has been incredibly popular with Rossi's customers, as Melburnians can't get enough of limoncello and lemony drinks generally. "Limoncello sales have nearly tripled in the past year in Melbourne," he says. "The D'oro Fizz is very elegant and classy, while still being approachable in terms of flavor—it's a crowd favorite that the regular punter will enjoy rather than a mixologist's cocktail made for mixologists, if you know what I mean, and that's very Melbourne. I think the beautiful aesthetic of the drink also plays a part—topped off with edible gold leaf, it's a showstopper!"

GLASSWARE: Collins glass

GARNISH: Gold leaf

- 1½ oz. | 45 ml Tommy's Limoncello
- ½ oz. | 15 ml Three Foxes Vodka
- 1 oz. | 30 ml fresh lemon juice
- ½ oz. | 15 ml simple syrup
- 3 drops Wonderfoam Cocktail Foamer
- Limonata, to top

1. Chill a collins glass. Combine all of the ingredients, except for the limonata, in a cocktail shaker and dry-shake (without ice).
2. Add ice and wet-shake.
3. Strain the cocktail into the chilled glass.
4. Slowly add the limonata then garnish with the gold leaf on the top.

FILIPPO RICCI, D.O.C GASTRONOMIA ITALIA ST KILDA

Melbourne is home to Australia's largest Italian community, and D.O.C has played a key role in developing the city's contemporary Italian dining scene since it opened its first venue in Carlton in 1997. D.O.C now has venues in Carlton, Mornington, Sydney, Southbank, and St Kilda.

Bar manager Filippo Ricci says the concept behind D.O.C St Kilda was to create a venue that celebrates Italian tradition while embracing its cultural progression—the very best of old and new. Located near the seaside, the restaurant's cocktail menu features Italian classics such as the Negroni and Aperol Spritz, alongside its signature cocktail, the St Kilda. "D.O.C has five signature cocktails, created to honor the five cities where we have restaurant venues," Ricci explains.

ST KILDA

D.O.C ST KILDA
14-16 THE ESPLANADE, ST KILDA

The St Kilda is a tribute to the excitement and vibrance of the local community, with a subtle nod to their unsubtle beach culture. It is as inherently Melbourne as it gets," says bar manager Filippo Ricci. He advises always using fresh lime juice and fresh ice when mixing the drink. "It's important to make sure that all flavors, including homemade components like shrubs, maintain their quality. While the shrub can be prepared in advance, it should be stored in the fridge to ensure the quality isn't adversely affected."

GLASSWARE: Highball glass

GARNISH: Watermelon triangle

- Black salt, for the rim
- 1 oz. | 30 ml Espolòn Tequila Blanco
- ⅓ oz. | 10 ml fresh lime juice
- ⅔ oz. | 20 ml Watermelon Shrub (see recipe)
- Fever-Tree Sparkling Pink Grapefruit, to top

1. Create a half rim with black salt around your highball glass.
2. Build the drink over ice in the order of ingredients listed.
3. Top with the pink grapefruit soda.
4. Garnish with a watermelon triangle.

WATERMELON SHRUB: Combine 34 oz. (1 liter) fresh watermelon juice, 1¼ lbs. (600 grams) white sugar, and 5 oz. (150 ml) apple cider vinegar. Mix until combined and the shrub is ready to serve.

BEAUTY AND THE BEAST

FLOUR CHILD
1/77 ACLAND STREET, ST KILDA

Bar manager Lachlan Grant says the beauty of Flour Child is that it features an open bar with "nowhere to hide. This gives the customers the full experience of being able to get up close to see what really goes on behind what we would usually call the bar top, taking interaction to the next level," he explains. The Beauty and The Beast never fails to dazzle those who order it, with its bubble gum cloud, which aims to appeal to all the senses. "All it takes is for one person to see and smell the aroma from a table across from them, and it becomes a chain effect throughout the venue," Grant says. Flour Child uses a Flavour Blaster smoking gun to create a thick bubble gum–scented cloud around the cocktail while it is inside a cloche.

GLASSWARE: Nick & Nora glass
GARNISH: Bubble gum cloud, rose petals

- 1 oz. | 30 ml Absolut Vodka
- 1 oz. | 30 ml Absolut Raspberri Vodka
- ⅔ oz. | 20 ml fresh lemon juice
- ⅔ oz. | 20 ml strawberry puree
- ¼ oz. | 7.5 ml simple syrup
- ⅓ oz. | 10 ml Monin Rose Syrup
- Wonderfoam Cocktail Foamer, to taste

1. Combine all of the ingredients in a Boston shaker with ice and shake.
2. Double-strain the cocktail into a Nick & Nora.
3. Garnish with a bubble gum cloud and rose petals.

HUW GRIFFITHS, UNION ELECTRIC

Union Electric describes itself as a cheeky little laneway cocktail bar and rooftop serving the finest cocktails, craft beers, gin, rum, loud shirts, and old-school hip-hop.

According to owner Huw Griffiths, the bar is a favorite with locals because the staff take their craft—but certainly not themselves—seriously and try their best to provide a great atmosphere in which to sip top-class drinks "without the hoity-toity bartender clichés," says Griffiths. "Customers love the laid-back vibe, fruit-forward cocktail flavors, music, and quintessentially Melbourne laneway setting," he says. The atmospheric venue also took out a spot on the world's Top 500 Bars list in 2023.

LOLA

Owner Huw Griffiths says Melbourne is a melting pot of cultures and the Lola cocktail aims to reflect that by bringing together flavors from all over the world. Lola was one of the earliest cocktails to feature on the bar's menu and Huw says it has stood the test of time due to being a beautifully balanced drink, approachable to everyone, good in any weather, and the fact it's hard to stop at just one! It's so good that Jamie Oliver even made it on his show," he says. The cocktail was invented by bartender Simon Eales and named after The Kinks, classic song, "Lola." Using Coco López is essential when making the cocktail; replacing it with an alternate coconut cream will not produce the required consistency and taste.

GLASSWARE: Double rocks glass
GARNISH: Cracked black pepper, orange twist, flower

- 1½ oz. | 45 ml London dry gin
- 1 oz. | 30 ml Coco López Cream of Coconut
- ½ oz. | 15 ml fresh lemon juice
- ⅓ oz. | 10 ml dry curaçao
- 1 teaspoon | 5 ml ginger puree

1. Combine all of the ingredients in a cocktail shaker and shake.
2. Dirty-dump (don't strain) the cocktail into a double rocks glass.
3. Garnish with freshly cracked black pepper, an orange twist, and flowers.

HOUSE HEMINGWAY DAIQUIRI

LOLA BELLE
233 BRUNSWICK STREET, FITZROY

Lola Belle is housed in a building constructed during the gold rush in the 1860s, when Melbourne briefly claimed the title of the world's richest city. At that time rum was currency in Australia and exotic new ingredients were arriving in the city en masse. Rums from around the world are a focus for Lola Belle, and general manager Lachy Hunter says the bar's Daiquiri menu pays tribute to that exciting time in Australia's history. The House Hemingway Daiquiri is also a nod to the local Fitzroy artists and writers that bring the suburb to life. Perfected by the bar's resident cocktail expert Jack Sandeman, it is a balanced, well-rounded drink that's not too sharp nor too sweet or boozy. Sandeman says acidifying the grapefruit juice is essential to balance the drink and prevent it from oxidizing too quickly.

GLASSWARE: Coupe glass
GARNISH: Grapefruit zest

- 1¾ oz. | 50 ml Planteray 3 Stars Rum
- ⅔ oz. | 20 ml Acidified Grapefruit Juice (see recipe)
- ½ oz. | 15 ml Grapefruit Syrup (see recipe)
- 1 teaspoon | 5 ml maraschino liqueur
- 4 drops saline solution
- 4 drops hopped grapefruit bitters

1. Chill a coupe glass. Combine all of the ingredients in a Boston shaker with ice and shake.
2. Double-strain the cocktail into the chilled coupe and garnish with grapefruit zest.

ACIDIFIED GRAPEFRUIT JUICE: Per 34 oz. (1 liter) grapefruit juice, add 13 grams malic acid and 27 grams citric acid and stir until the powders are dissolved.

GRAPEFRUIT SYRUP: Combine equal parts by weight freshly strained grapefruit juice and white sugar. Stir until the sugar is dissolved.

SOEREN POULSEN, STARWARD DISTILLERY & BAR

Starward Distillery was established in 2007 in a former Qantas maintenance hangar at Essendon Airport by founder David Vitale. Decades later it is one of Australia's foremost whiskey producers, with Starward Distillery & Bar recently reopening in the heart of Port Melbourne, featuring a renovation that blends a modern industrial aesthetic with a welcoming ambience.

Starward bar manager Soeren Poulsen says the distillery's whiskies are perfect for both sipping and mixing. "I always recommend drinking Starward how you like it; if that's with a mixer then go for gold!" he says.

One of his personal favorite combinations is Starward Two-Fold and apple juice. However, he advises that his general rule of thumb is that the bigger the ABV, the less likely he is to add a mixer.

TWO PASSIONS

STARWARD DISTILLERY & BAR
50 BERTIE STREET, PORT MELBOURNE

The Two Passions was inspired by a popular Australian dessert, the pavlova. "Whenever we create new cocktails here at Starward, we always keep in mind Melbourne's great love of fantastic foods and tasty desserts," says bar manager Soeren Poulsen. "This cocktail heroes our versatile and approachable Two-Fold Whisky, which is fully matured in red wine barrels, meaning it's got a delicious profile of juicy red fruits and berries. It really is the perfect base for this cocktail and perfectly complements its fruity and vanilla-forward flavors." When it comes to making a Sour, Poulsen says it's all about the foam. "What you're after is a silky, smooth foam, not too thick, not too thin," he advises. "A good dry shake before or after shaking with ice will really help emulsify the ingredients and give you that superb mouthfeel."

GLASSWARE: Coupette glass

GARNISH: Spray of peated whisky

- 1¾ oz. | 50 ml Starward Two-Fold Whisky
- 1 oz. | 30 ml fresh lemon juice
- ⅔ oz. | 20 ml Passion Fruit & Vanilla Syrup (see recipe)
- 1 egg white

1. Chill a coupette. Combine all of the ingredients in a cocktail shaker and dry-shake (without ice).

2. Add ice and shake again.

3. Double-strain the cocktail into the chilled coupette.

4. Garnish with a spritz of peated whiskey.

PASSION FRUIT & VANILLA SYRUP: In a container, combine 1 barspoon passion fruit pulp, 3 drops of vanilla extract, and ⅔ oz. (20 ml) simple syrup and stir to combine. Strain.

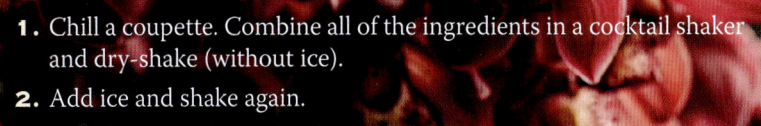

STRAWBERRY SHORTCAKE

STARWARD DISTILLERY & BAR
50 BERTIE STREET, PORT MELBOURNE

S tarward is one of Australia's most-awarded distilleries and took home thirteen Double Gold medals, eight Platinum medals and thirteen Gold Medals at the 2024 San Francisco World Spirits Competition. This delicious cocktail highlights one of its Double Gold–winning whiskies, Nova.

GLASSWARE: Coupe glass

GARNISH: Freeze-dried strawberries, crushed; strawberry wafer cookies

- 1⅓ oz. | 40 ml Strawberry-Infused Nova (see recipe)
- ⅓ oz. | 10 ml strawberry syrup
- ⅓ oz. | 10 ml verjus
- 1 oz. | 30 ml Vanilla-Infused Cream (see recipe)

1. Combine all of the ingredients, except for the cream, in a mixing glass with ice and stir.
2. Strain the cocktail into a coupe.
3. Layer the cream on top.
4. Garnish with crushed freeze-dried strawberries and serve with strawberry wafer cookies.

STRAWBERRY-INFUSED NOVA: Make 30 grams T2 Tea Strawberries & Cream Tea according to the instructions on the packet and allow the tea to cool to room temperature. Add the tea to 3⅓ oz. (100 ml) Starward Nova Whisky, and let the mixture sit for 10 minutes then double-strain.

VANILLA-INFUSED CREAM:
Combine 1 cup heavy whipping cream and 1 teaspoon vanilla extract in the bowl of an electric mixer fitted with the whisk attachment. Beat the cream until peaks form.

(NEW) OLD FASHIONED

The (New) Old Fashioned is a modern take on the classic whiskey cocktail, subbing in agave nectar instead of simple syrup and grapefruit peel in place of orange peel.

GLASSWARE: Rocks glass

GARNISH: Cherry and grapefruit peel on a skewer

- 2 oz. | 60 ml Starward Nova Whisky
- Agave nectar, to taste
- 2 to 3 dashes bitters

1. Combine all of the ingredients in a mixing glass with ice and stir.
2. Strain the cocktail into a rocks glass over a large ice rock.
3. Garnish with a skewered cherry and grapefruit peel.

BEESPRESSO MARTINI

PUSS & MEW DISTILLERY
I VARMAN COURT, NUNAWADING

The bar at Puss & Mew Distillery has a speakeasy feel, with a mixture of Chesterfield couches and cozy English pub chairs and tables. The unique setting includes a bespoke botanical wall and the distillery's alembic stills on show. Melbourne is the coffee capital of Australia and the heartland of its favorite cocktail, the Espresso Martini. Puss & Mew director Debra Clayton says the distillery's award-winning Honey Coconut Gin and a splash of honey syrup take the classic cocktail to the next level.

GLASSWARE: Champagne coupe glass

GARNISH: 3 coffee beans; honeycomb, crushed

- 1½ oz. | 45 ml Puss & Mew Honey Coconut Gin
- 1 oz. | 30 ml coffee liqueur
- 1 oz. | 30 ml espresso
- ½ oz. | 15 ml Honey Syrup (see recipe)

1. Combine all of the ingredients in a cocktail shaker with ice and shake hard for 10 to 15 seconds.
2. Double-strain the cocktail into a champagne coupe glass.
3. Garnish with 3 coffee beans and a sprinkle of crushed honeycomb.

HONEY SYRUP: In a container, combine 1 cup honey and 1 cup hot water and stir. Allow the syrup to cool.

HARSHIL VORA, STRATO MELBOURNE

Bartender Harshil Vora says there's nothing quite like the wow factor of arriving at Strato Melbourne, which is located on the fortieth floor of the Oakwood Premiere Melbourne hotel. The venue boasts a sixteen-meter stone bar with an illuminated glass-brick frame alongside an alfresco terrace with a view that resembles the skyline of New York City.

Tall glass windows allow guests to enjoy the skyline while sampling appetizers, seasonal cocktails, wines, and craft beers. "Strato provides a bucket-list experience," Vora says. "In addition to its extraordinary views reaching far over Port Phillip Bay, across the Yarra River, CBD skyline, and beyond, Strato Melbourne provides guests with an all-encompassing, quintessential Melbourne experience."

THE MONKEY MANGO

S trato Melbourne bartender Harshil Vora describes The Monkey Mango as being more than just a cocktail—it is a voyage in a glass to the heart of Southeast Asia while in the middle of Melbourne. "It was during such an exploration that the vision for the cocktail came to me. Walking through a lush grove, I encountered a playful scene—a cheeky monkey delighting in the sweet bounty of ripe mangoes under the cool shade of towering coconut trees. The air was rich with the scent of mangoes, while the whisper of the palm fronds composed a tranquil symphony." To create a harmonious blend of flavors, mix the mango puree with a splash of lime juice for a touch of acidity. This will counterbalance the sweetness of the mango and enhance the overall taste profile. Add a hint of cucumber juice for a refreshing twist that complements the richer mango and lime.

GLASSWARE: Belgian beer glass

GARNISH: Coconut cream foam, mint sprig, roasted coconut threads

- 4 cucumber slices
- 1½ oz. | 45 ml 1800 Coconut Tequila
- 1 oz. | 30 ml pineapple juice
- ⅔ oz. | 20 ml mango puree
- ½ oz. | 15 ml Feels Botanical Vivify
- ½ oz. | 15 ml fresh lime juice
- Pinch ground clove
- Pinch cardamom
- 4 mint leaves

1. In the bottom of a cocktail shaker, muddle the cucumber pieces.
2. Add the remaining ingredients with ice and shake vigorously.
3. Double-strain the cocktail over crushed ice into a Belgian glass.
4. Using a cream whipper, garnish the cocktail with a layer of coconut cream foam.
5. Garnish with a mint sprig and a sprinkle of roasted coconut threads.

CAPTAIN'S COVE COLADA

FLEET
LEVEL 22, 1 QUEEN STREET

Fleet bar manager Claire More says visitors, travelers, and Melburnians alike are drawn to the venue by its amazing views over the Yarra River, Port Phillip Bay, Southbank, and beyond, but they stay for the cozy vibes and extensive drinks list. Fleet's stylish travertine bar is generously stocked with more than seventy different rums from around the world. A vintage and rare bottle collection, dating back to the 1930s, completes the rum offering. "The Captain's Cove Colada is an old-school Piña Colada. Our customers love a bit of nostalgia with a touch of excitement," More says.

GLASSWARE: Collins glass

GARNISH: Pandan leaf, maraschino cherry

- 2 oz. | 60 ml JimmyRum Navy
- 1 oz. | 30 ml fresh pineapple juice
- ⅔ oz. | 20 ml Pineapple & Lime Cordial (see recipe)
- ½ oz. | 15 ml Toasted Coconut Syrup (see recipe)
- ½ oz. | 15 ml Pandan Distillate (see recipe)

1. Chill a collins glass. Combine all of the ingredients with ice in a cocktail shaker and shake.
2. Double-strain the cocktail into the chilled collins glass.
3. Add ice and garnish with a fresh pandan leaf and maraschino cherry.

PINEAPPLE & LIME CORDIAL: Make an oleo-saccharum with pineapple skins, lime peels, and 1 lb. (500 grams) sugar. After 12 hours, add 15 oz. (450 ml) pineapple juice, 1¾ oz. (50 ml) fresh lime juice, and a pinch of citric acid. When all of the sugar has dissolved, strain out the peels.

TOASTED COCONUT SYRUP: In a skillet over medium heat, toast coconut flakes, to taste, on medium heat until they are caramelized. Using a 2:1 ratio, in a small saucepan over low heat, combine demerara sugar and water and stir until the sugar is dissolved. Add the toasted coconut flakes and leave the syrup to infuse for 6 hours, then strain.

PANDAN DISTILLATE: Fleet is fortunate enough to have a Rotavapor on-site, but the distillate can also be created by sous vide, it just takes a little longer. Infuse fresh pandan leaves, as needed, with the white spirit of your choice.

REDUCE, REDRINK, RECYCLE

The Q has become a go-to rooftop destination for zesty Southeast Asian bites and delicious cocktails, served with a side of Melbourne skyline. All drinks at The Q are vegan, with aquafaba used as an egg white alternative. To keep waste at a minimum, The Q is also creative with any fruit that may be leftover, using it to make syrups or garnishes. Beverage manager Hugh Hamilton explains how the Reduce, Redrink, Recycle cocktail was concocted to use lime husks and finger lime skins from the kitchen in a syrup. They are combined with Brookies Pacific Moonshine, which itself was concocted by distilling wasted beer from a nearby brewery during one of Melbourne's COVID-19 lockdowns. "Finger lime is a native Australian fruit known for its burst of tangy citrus flavor," says Hamilton, "adding a distinctive twist to your cocktail."

GLASSWARE: Nick & Nora glass

GARNISH: Kaffir lime leaf, dehydrated orange wheel

- 1⅓ oz. | 40 ml Havana Club Añejo 3 Años
- 1 oz. | 30 ml fresh lime juice
- ⅔ oz. | 20 ml Brookies Pacific Moonshine
- ½ oz. | 15 ml "Recycle" Syrup (see recipe)

1. Combine all of the ingredients in a cocktail shaker with ice and shake vigorously.

2. Strain the cocktail into a Nick & Nora and garnish with a kaffir lime leaf and dehydrated orange wheel.

"RECYCLE" SYRUP: In a saucepan over medium-low heat, cook leftover lime husks, the skins of finger limes, and kaffir leaves with equal amounts of sugar and water, stirring, until the sugar is dissolved. Strain the syrup and let it cool.

MICHAEL MADRUSAN, *THE EVERLEIGH*

Founder Michael Madrusan worked at New York City's famed Milk & Honey bar for six years before returning to Melbourne to open The Everleigh in 2011. The intimate neighborhood venue celebrates the golden age of classic cocktails in surroundings full of speakeasy charm. Michael says The Everleigh isn't an "order-taking bar."

"It listens, it suggests. The Everleigh gets to know you and what it is you really love," he says. "Every moment at the table is a chance to get to know your guests better, and with that, it gives us a chance to deliver a tailored experience they love and remember."

LA BESTIA

L a Bestia was inspired by Melburnians' love affair with both coffee and tequila. "That's what makes this drink a hit—consider it the ultimate dessert cocktail," The Everleigh's founder, Michael Madrusan, says.

GLASSWARE: Coupette glass

- 1½ oz. | 45 ml blanco tequila

- 1½ oz. | 45 ml coffee liqueur
- Hand-Whipped Cream (see recipe), to top

1. Freeze a coupette glass. In a mixing glass with ice, stir down the tequila and coffee liqueur.

2. Strain the cocktail into the frozen coupette.

3. Gently pour your fresh whipped cream on top.

HAND-WHIPPED CREAM: Add 3 oz. (90 ml) of double cream to a cocktail shaker with 1 sugar cube. Shake until the cream is thick and fluffy and the cube is dissolved, about 20 seconds.

WATERMELON GARIBALDI

The cocktail menu at Rocco's Bologna Discoteca is succinct and finely tuned. "I think having a limited cocktail menu forces people to broaden their horizons and experience flavors they're not normally used to," says beverage director Alex Pineo. "Cutting the fat of prepping every classic cocktail lets us be creative and do a few signature cocktails really well." A star ingredient in the Watermelon Garibaldi is Saison Rhubarb Vermouth, which is made in Melbourne by Embla wine bar owner Dave Verheul, while the watermelon juice is sourced from Market Juice in the historic Queen Victoria Market, a produce market that has been operating in the city since 1878. "Saison Rhubarb Vermouth is such an approachable vermouth to start people off with if they are unfamiliar with the spirit and provides the Robin to the watermelon juice's Batman," Pineo says.

GLASSWARE: Rocks glass

GARNISH: Sea salt

- 3 oz. | 90 ml fresh watermelon juice
- 1½ oz. | 45 ml Saison Rhubarb Vermouth

1. Combine the juice and vermouth in a cocktail shaker with ice and shake.
2. Strain the cocktail into a rocks glass with a large cube of ice.
3. Garnish with a pinch of sea salt on top.

BARB

Poodle Bar and Bistro bar manager Zii Diggles says the Barb is an unusual and daring drink, with taste sensations that sing together harmoniously. "It's a Pink Negroni, with a creative Melbourne twist, leaving you wanting more," Diggles says. Using an ice rock will ensure that the cocktail maintains the perfect dilution for its delicate flavors. A small pinch of salt on top of the cube is all that is needed to emphasize the saline within the rhubarb-based alcohol.

GLASSWARE: Rocks glass

GARNISH: Sea salt, fennel sprig

- 1 oz. | 30 ml Saison Rhubarb Vermouth
- 1 oz. | 30 ml RHUBI Mistelle
- 1 oz. | 30 ml Tanqueray London Dry Gin

1. Combine all of the ingredients in a mixing glass with plenty of ice and stir.
2. Double-strain the cocktail into a rocks glass with a large cube of ice.
3. Garnish the ice cube with a pinch of sea salt and add a sprig of fennel to the glass.

CHRIS GAWEDA, ROOFTOP AT QT

Rooftop at QT Melbourne offers its customers a unique experience that combines panoramic views of the city's skyline with innovative cocktails in a bustling, vibrant atmosphere.

"We are always striving to exceed the ordinary with our carefully crafted signature food and drink offerings," says beverage director Chris Gaweda. "We are inspired by local flavors and push the boundaries, breathing life into old and new concepts, taking inspiration from our team, culture, and surroundings." Chris has been mixing cocktails at QT for more than six years after initially entering hospitality as a side hustle while he was studying. "However, as time went on, I'd often find myself between shifts dreaming up different cocktail mixes and jotting down winning flavor combinations to experiment with." From the creativity in his role to the enjoyment of interacting with customers, he says, "Life behind the bar is an adult's playground."

Q-TEA SOUR

Customers love how well the flavors of the spirits pair with the tea syrup in the Q-Tea Sour. "During the summer season, the Q-Tea Sour was one of our highest-selling drinks on the menu," beverage director Chris Gaweda says. "It also has a lot of visual appeal—it's vibrant, contrasting, and theatrical in its design. People drink with their eyes first, so it's no surprise how popular the drink was for us." QT teamed up with Australian Distilling Co. to hero its Rhapsody Ruby Gin, which uses elderberries, black currant, hibiscus, rosehip, and apple to create a beautiful, sweet spirit that pairs perfectly with the bar's house-brewed tea.

GLASSWARE: Coupette glass

GARNISH: Raspberry powder, dehydrated rose petals

- 1 oz. | 30 ml Australian Distilling Co. Rhapsody Ruby Gin

- ⅓ oz. | 10 ml Bulldog London Dry Gin

- ⅓ oz. | 10 ml Unico Rosa Rosé Vermouth

- ⅓ oz. | 10 ml Aperol

- 2 oz. | 60 ml Earl Grey & Lavender Tea Syrup (see recipe)

- ⅔ oz. | 20 ml fresh lemon juice

- 1 fresh raspberry

- 5 drops aquafaba

1. Combine the gins, vermouth, Aperol, tea syrup, and lemon juice in a cocktail shaker without ice, then add the raspberry and aquafaba.

2. Dry-shake, then add ice and wet-shake.

3. Double-strain the cocktail into a coupette.

4. Garnish with raspberry powder and dehydrated rose petals across the top.

EARL GREY & LAVENDER TEA SYRUP: Steep 4 grams lavender bulbs in 3½ oz. (100 ml) boiling water for 30 minutes then let it cool to room temperature. In a separate container, steep 7.5 grams Earl Grey tea leaves in 10 oz. (300 ml) boiling water for 30 minutes and let it cool to room temperature. In a third container, mix 5 oz. (150 ml) honey with 5 oz. (150 ml) boiling water. Strain both tea concentrates together into a new container, and add 13½ oz. (400 ml) cold water to the tea mixture to extend the volume and soften the flavors. Mix the honey water into the tea water to finalize the batch.

RUMBLESTRIP

Pascale Bar & Grill, located on Level One of QT Melbourne, creates innovative seasonal cocktails crafted with local botanicals. "From curious to classic, every drink is exquisite, matching any mood," says beverage director Chris Gaweda. The Rumblestrip was launched for the Formula 1 Rolex Australian Grand Prix 2024, which drew hundreds of thousands of people to Melbourne's Albert Park Grand Prix Circuit. The cocktail was created to capture the city's fast-paced action and bustling nightlife, bringing the excitement of the Grand Prix off the track.

GLASSWARE: Wineglass

GARNISH: Orange twist

- 1¾ oz. | 50 ml Idle Hour Rye Vodka
- 1 oz. | 30 ml mandarin juice
- 17/20 oz. | 25 ml cranberry juice
- ⅓ oz. | 10 ml Cointreau
- ⅓ oz. | 10 ml fresh lime juice

1. Combine all of the ingredients in a cocktail shaker with ice and shake.
2. Strain the cocktail into a wineglass.
3. Garnish with an orange twist.

THE LAMINGTON

The Douglas Club is located inside Hilton Melbourne Little Queen Street, set within the historic Equity Chambers Building. Head bartender Brandon Linsley says patrons love The Douglas Club's personal approach. "Creating a cocktail-centric community is what makes it all worthwhile—the design of the bar, the shapes, the feel of the leather couches, our kaleidoscopic artwork combined with funk, disco, and jazz. It's a filling experience." The Lamington was inspired by a traditional Australian cake made from squares of sponge cake with a layer of jam in the middle, coated in chocolate sauce and rolled in desiccated coconut. Linsley has four tips for serving it perfectly: Make sure your glassware is fresh out of the fridge or freezer; don't stir the drink too much, as it will mature in the glass; use large ice cubes to slow dilution; and make the jam fresh from your favorite berries. This batch recipe makes ten serves.

GLASSWARE: Rocks glass

GARNISH: Fresh raspberries on a skewer

- 15¼ oz. | 450 ml aged rum
- 5 oz. | 150 ml coconut rum
- 11 tablespoons | 150 grams cacao butter

- 10 oz. | 300 ml sweet red vermouth
- 5 tablespoons | 150 grams mixed berry jam

1. In one vacuum-sealable bag, combine the rums and cacao butter, and in a second bag combine the vermouth and jam. Seal both bags.

2. Sous vide the bags at 175°F (80°C) for 3 hours. Then place both bags in the refrigerator overnight.

3. Strain the contents of each bag separately through muslin cloth in a fine-mesh strainer. Then bottle and store them separately in the refrigerator until ready to use.

4. To serve, combine them 2:1 rum mixture to jam mixture in a rocks glass over a large ice rock.

5. Garnish with fresh raspberries on a skewer.

CHRIS HYSTED-ADAMS, MOON DOG WILD WEST

Melbourne craft brewer Moon Dog's newest venue, Moon Dog Wild West, is set in a historic building in the heart of the vibrant suburb of Footscray. The cocktail menu is carefully curated by three-time Australian Bartender of the Year Chris Hysted-Adams, who describes himself as the brewery's "flavourologist." Chris was at the helm of Melbourne's Black Pearl when it won Best International Cocktail bar at the 2017 Spirited Awards and is famed for creating the modern cocktail classic the Death Flip. Hysted-Adams mixed his first Death Flip in 2010, a daring combination of Chartreuse, tequila, Jägermeister, and a whole egg.

"You know how it is," he explains. "You're a young, impressionable bartender, so all you like drinking is tequila, Jägermeister, and Chartreuse. You also love drinking any cocktails that have tequila, Jägermeister, or Chartreuse in them. Chances are, during service, you're recommending cocktails to your guests with tequila, Jägermeister, or Chartreuse in them."

Frustrated by customers' reluctance to try his favorite spirits, he decided to concoct the intriguingly named Death Flip. No ingredients were listed on the menu, as Hysted-Adams wanted people to leave their preconceptions at the door. When customers asked him what it contained, he would infamously reply: "You don't wanna meet this cocktail in a dark alley." It didn't take long for the Death Flip to develop a cult following and start appearing on cocktail lists across the globe. Almost fifteen years later, Chris still gets requests to mix the iconic cocktail, although he admits he leans more toward sipping Tommy's Margaritas or Moon Dog seltzers these days.

WILD WEST BLOODY MARY

MOON DOG WILD WEST
54 HOPKINS STREET, FOOTSCRAY

Moon Dog Wild West spans three levels and boasts more than a hundred beer taps. Patrons enter through swinging saloon doors on the ground floor, where a bucking bull stands strong as the centerpiece. Moon Dog flavourologist Chris Hysted-Adams says the cocktail is a favorite with patrons because it matches so well with the American-style food on the menu. "It's also absolutely perfect for a Melburnian's favorite weekend activity—brunch," he says. "This Bloody Mary is so good, I *want* to feel dusty to enjoy it even more."

GLASSWARE: Mason jar

GARNISH: 1 pickle and 1 large pickled Guindilla pepper on a skewer

- **Old Bay seasoning, as needed, for the rim, plus 1 teaspoon**
- **1¾ oz. | 50 ml vodka**
- **5 oz. | 150 ml tomato juice**
- **½ oz. | 15 ml barbecue sauce**
- **⅓ oz. | 10 ml fresh lemon juice**
- **1 tablespoon Worcestershire sauce**

1. Dip the rim of a mason jar in water then dip it in Old Bay seasoning. Build the cocktail by adding the ingredients in the order listed in the rimmed mason jar.

2. Stir briefly and add ice.

3. Garnish with a pickle and large pickled Guindilla pepper skewered together.

BREAK FREE!

BACKROOM
234 TOORAK ROAD, SOUTH YARRA

Backroom is a basement bar hidden inside the Ovolo South Yarra hotel. Head bartender Darlan Alves focused on upcycling when creating the Break Free! cocktail. "We're taking overlooked ingredients like plantains from the kitchen and giving them a new life in a delicious drink," he says. "It's a creative way to use what we already have, and it's a perfect fit for the cocktail's flavor profile. If you are vegan, swap the honey syrup for orgeat."

GLASSWARE: Martini glass

GARNISH: Fried plantain chip

- 2 oz. | 60 ml dry gin
- 1 oz. | 30 ml fresh lemon juice
- ⅔ oz. | 20 ml banana puree
- ½ oz. | 15 ml honey syrup

1. Chill a martini glass. Combine all of the ingredients in a cocktail shaker with ice and shake vigorously for 10 to 15 seconds.
2. Double-strain the cocktail into the chilled martini glass
3. Garnish with a crispy fried plantain slice.

NAUGHT SATURN

NAUGHT COCKTAIL BAR
2/32 PEEL STREET, ELTHAM

G arnished with a smoke-filled bubble, this is one of the most pho-
tographed cocktails on our menu," says operations manager
Connor Heffernan, who recommends freezing the glassware for thirty
minutes before serving.

GLASSWARE: Coupe glass

GARNISH: Passion fruit–smoke-filled bubble or lemon twist

- 1¾ oz. | 50 ml Naught Australian Dry Gin
- 17/20 oz. | 25 ml fresh lemon juice
- ½ oz. | 15m passion fruit syrup
- ⅓ oz. | 10 ml Falernum
- ⅓ oz. | 10 ml orgeat

1. Chill a coupe glass. Combine all of the ingredients in a cocktail shaker with ice and shake vigorously for 15 seconds.

2. Double-strain the cocktail into a chilled coupe.

3. Garnish with a passion fruit–smoke-filled bubble or a lemon twist.

FLAMINGO

ATRIUM BAR
CROWN MELBOURNE, 8 WHITEMAN STREET,
SOUTHBANK

Atrium Bar manager Matt Amos says the pizzazz of the Flamingo lies in the use of fresh fruit and its vibrant pink color, which appeals to patrons seeking social media moments. "It's like street art in a glass, combined with the freshness of fruit picked from the Queen Victoria Market," he says. He advises that the fresher the fruit, the better the taste.

GLASSWARE: Double rocks glass

GARNISH: Rosemary sprig, dehydrated grapefruit half-moon

- 1½ oz. | 45 ml Strawberry, Rhubarb, and Apple Syrup (see recipe)
- 1 oz. | 30 ml Ketel One Vodka
- 1 oz. | 30 ml De Kuyper Wild Strawberry Liqueur
- ¼ oz. | 15 ml fresh lime juice
- Dash rhubarb bitters

1. Combine all of the ingredients in a cocktail shaker with ice and shake.
2. Strain the cocktail over ice into a double rocks glass.
3. Garnish with rosemary and a dehydrated grapefruit half-moon.

STRAWBERRY, RHUBARB, AND APPLE SYRUP: In a container, combine (500 ml) juiced strawberries, (250 ml) fresh apple juice, (100 ml) rhubarb juice and stir. Strain the mixture through a fine-mesh strainer into a saucepan over medium-low heat, and add 100 grams brown sugar. Stir until the sugar dissolves and simmer until the mixture thickens, about 10 to 15 minutes. Allow the syrup to cool.

PASH & SMASH

GING THAI
CROWN MELBOURNE, 8 WHITEMAN STREET,
SOUTHBANK

A collision of sweet and sour, the combination of lush passion fruit, spicy chile, and fresh Thai basil in the Pash & Smash results in a well-balanced cocktail that celebrates the excitement of Thailand.

GLASSWARE: Highball glass

GARNISH: Thai basil leaves

- 1½ oz. | 45 ml gin
- ⅔ oz. | 20 ml passion fruit puree
- ⅔ oz. | 20 ml fresh lime juice
- ½ oz. | 15 ml Cointreau
- 5 Thai basil leaves
- 1 small slice of Thai green chile

1. Combine all of the ingredients in a cocktail shaker with ice and shake.

2. Strain the cocktail into a highball filled with crushed ice.

3. Garnish with fresh Thai basil and serve.

PURPLE RAIN

FIDELS
CROWN MELBOURNE, 8 WHITEMAN STREET,
SOUTHBANK

Fidels aims to transport patrons to the lively streets of Havana in the heart of Melbourne. The venue features color-drenched decor, Latin music, and an outdoor terrace that provides the perfect setting to sip on cocktails as you soak up the city lights. Restaurant manager Emma O'Connell says the Purple Rain was inspired by the nightlife on the Crown Riverwalk that winds past the bar. "The drink's color draws the crowds in, while the well-balanced sweet and sour aromas keep them coming back," she says. She recommends topping with soda if you prefer to offset the sweetness.

GLASSWARE: Collins glass

GARNISH: Dehydrated orange wheel

- 1 oz. | 30 ml Ketel One Vodka
- 1 oz. | 30 ml Alizé Gold Passion
- 1 oz. | 30 ml simple syrup
- 1 oz. | 30 ml fresh lemon juice
- ½ oz. | 15 ml Raspberry Cordial (see recipe)
- Soda water, to top

1. Chill a collins glass. Combine all of the ingredients, except for the soda, in a cocktail shaker with ice and shake.

2. Double-strain the cocktail into the chilled collins glass over crushed ice.

3. Top with soda water.

4. Garnish with a dehydrated orange wheel.

RASPBERRY CORDIAL: In a small saucepan over medium-low heat, combine 250 grams fresh raspberries, 125 grams superfine (caster) sugar, and the zest of 1 lime and bring the mixture to a simmer, stirring until the sugar is dissolved and mashing the berries. Cook for about 20 minutes and then allow the mixture to cool. Stir in the juice of 1 lime. Fine-strain the cordial into a sterilized bottle.

KAIMU

The Kaimu has a complex flavor profile that balances sweet and spicy notes. Its finishing touch is a fragrant smoked cinnamon stick, which enhances the overall sensory experience while complementing the other ingredients. "The cozy warmth from the cinnamon symbolizes a comforting escape from Melbourne's occasional cold snaps," restaurant manager Gaurav Khanna says. For best results, age the ingredients in an oak barrel for a minimum of three days to promote character.

GLASSWARE: Rocks glass

GARNISH: Flamed cinnamon stick

- 1 oz. | 30 ml Kraken Black Spiced Rum
- ⅓ oz. | 10 ml apricot brandy
- ⅓ oz. | 10 ml cinnamon syrup
- 2 dashes chocolate bitters
- ⅓ oz. | 10 ml Laphroaig 10

1. Combine all of the ingredients, except for the whiskey, in a mixing glass and quick-stir with ice cubes.

2. Strain the cocktail over a large cube of ice into a rocks glass.

3. Float a barspoon of whiskey over the drink.

4. Garnish with a smoking cinnamon stick.

EL BURRO

Ghost Donkey serves craft cocktails made with traditional Mexican spirits and artisanal brands. The lively, vibrant bar features more than thirty-five mezcals and tequilas on its menu. El Burro is presented in a kitsch donkey cup decorated with seasonal flowers. Venue manager Vijay Velusamy describes the drink as a "sensory whirlwind," adding, "Mirroring the delicious diversity of Melbourne itself, it's more than just a tasty beverage; it's a stand-alone work of art."

GLASSWARE: Ceramic vessel

GARNISH: Fresh flower, parasol

- ⅔ oz. | 20 ml pineapple juice
- ½ oz. | 15 ml agave nectar
- ⅓ oz. | 10 ml Ilegal Mezcal Joven
- ⅓ oz. | 10 ml 1800 Coconut Tequila
- ⅓ oz. | 10 ml Planteray Stiggins' Fancy Pineapple Rum
- ⅓ oz. | 10 ml Planteray O.F.T.D. Overproof Rum
- ⅓ oz. | 10 ml orange juice
- ⅓ oz. | 10 ml passion fruit puree
- ⅓ oz. | 10 ml fresh lime juice
- 1 teaspoon | 5 ml Campari

1. Combine all of the ingredients in a cocktail shaker with ice and shake.
2. Strain the cocktail over ice with a crushed ice cap.
3. Garnish with fresh flowers and a parasol.

SLOE GIN SOUR

TWR
CROWN MELBOURNE, 8 WHITEMAN STREET,
SOUTHBANK

Dressed in a plush ensemble of dark timber, black granite, burnished brass features, bronze mirror paneling, and sweeping velvet curtains, TWR is a lush destination for elevated occasions. The bar's Sloe Gin Sour is a quintessential summer Sour, balancing contrasting elements and served in a delicate coupe. "This zesty drink evokes everyone's favorite memories of summer," says restaurant manager Andrew Ham.

GLASSWARE: Martini coupe glass
GARNISH: Rose petal

- 2 oz. | 60 ml sloe gin
- 1 oz. | 30 ml egg white
- ½ oz. | 15 ml elderflower syrup
- ½ oz. | 15 ml fresh lime juice
- ½ oz. | 15 ml orange juice

1. Combine all of the ingredients in a cocktail shaker without ice and dry-shake.
2. Add ice and wet-shake.
3. Double-strain the cocktail into a martini coupe.
4. Garnish with a single rose petal.

SMITHY

THE BLACKSMITH
69 SWAN STREET, RICHMOND

The Smithy is a versatile cocktail that hits the mark on all fronts. With its cucumber essence, it appeals to cocktail lovers seeking a refreshing sip. It also aims to delight whiskey enthusiasts while serving as an easy introduction to the spirit for those who may not consider themselves fans. The weather in Melbourne can infamously shift in an instant. The Smithy caters to the unpredictable climate—the whiskey provides a comforting warmth for chilly moments, while the cool cucumber and elderflower offer a refreshing respite from the heat. Make sure to muddle the cucumber well and strain out the small chunks after shaking—you don't want to chew your drink!

GLASSWARE: Rocks glass

GARNISH: Cucumber ribbon on a skewer

- 4 to 8 cucumber chunks
- 1½ oz. | 45 ml Glenfiddich 12 Year Old Single Malt Scotch Whisky
- ⅔ oz. | 20 ml fresh lemon juice
- ½ oz. | 15 ml Fiorente Elderflower Liqueur
- ½ oz. | 15 ml simple syrup

1. In a cocktail shaker, muddle the cucumber.
2. Add the remaining ingredients and ice and shake.
3. Double-strain the cocktail into a rocks glass and top with fresh ice.
4. Garnish with a skewered cucumber ribbon.

THE LAST WORD

Katuk boasts the largest collection of Chartreuse in Australia and The Last Word has been a firm favorite with the bar's patrons for the past seventeen years. The cocktail was created to echo the city's cultural richness, blending global influences into a harmonious sip.

GLASSWARE: Coupette glass

GARNISH: Maraschino cherry

- ⅔ oz. | 20 ml Beefeater Gin
- ⅔ oz. | 20 ml Green Chartreuse
- ⅔ oz. | 20 ml Luxardo Maraschino Originale
- ⅔ oz. | 20 ml fresh lime juice

1. Combine all of the ingredients in a cocktail shaker with ice and shake.
2. Add a maraschino cherry to a coupette and double-strain the cocktail into the coupette.

VODKA POUR OVER

LUI BAR
LEVEL 55, RIALTO TOWERS, 525 COLLINS STREET

The sensory journey at Lui Bar begins with the use of Australian materials throughout the venue, including granite, natural brass, sheepskin, and smoked glass, which come together to create a hyper-local built environment. Guests also love the bar for its stunning views, ambience, and, of course, great cocktails. The Vodka Pour Over has been on the menu since Lui Bar opened its doors in 2011. "Every now and then, we change the recipe, but the concept remains the same," says manager Elisabetta Lupi. "The way it is served is unique too—it's dripped into the glass while incorporating liquid nitrogen, creating a proper show. The cocktail is inspired by Melbourne's coffee culture. We wanted to pay homage to the city's great cafes." As the Vodka Pour Over is a Martini-style cocktail, a chilled coupette is a must—leave it in the freezer for at least ten minutes.

GLASSWARE: Coupette glass

- **17/20 oz. | 25 ml manzanilla sherry**
- **⅔ oz. | 20 ml Ketel One Vodka**
- **⅓ oz. | 10 ml violet liqueur**
- **⅓ oz. | 10 ml dark cacao**
- **⅓ oz. | 10 ml cocoa syrup**
- **1 teaspoon | 5 ml honey**
- **1 teaspoon freshly ground single origin coffee beans**

1. Chill a coupette. Fill a pour-over funnel with ice.
2. Add all of the ingredients to the funnel and place the funnel on top of the chilled coupette.
3. Let the liquid drip into the glass for approximately 1 minute, then remove the funnel to serve.

CORINA RETTER, LE MARTINI

Le Martini is the world's first standalone Grey Goose bar, created in partnership with Crown Melbourne. It is dedicated to both its name-sake and one of the world's best-known cocktails—the Martini. Guests at Le Martini are greeted by the intimate warmth and cozy feel of a speakeasy, evoked through Le Martini's plush velvet drapery and ban-quette seating in deep blue hues, softly curved bar, and subtle nods to the famous French vodka brand via aged mirrors etched with geese and opulent glass chandeliers. One of the creative forces behind the bar is the national brand ambassador for Grey Goose, Corina Retter.

Prior to joining Grey Goose, Corina spent almost two decades working in the Melbourne bar scene across a range of venues includ-ing Bar Margaux, Capitano, and Gimlet at Cavendish House. Accord-ing to Corina, the Martini is having a huge moment in bars throughout Melbourne. "House styles are taken very seriously, and true Martini aficionados take note of what they like best about each and every one

around the city," Retter says. "The Martini is a drink with a small number of in-gredients, but infinite possibilities—it relies on quality ingredients but also on the skill of the maker. In Mel-bourne we have a huge appreciation for quality and skill—just look at our coffee scene!"

In Melbourne, the quest to make the perfect Martini never stops. "As a Martini appreciator, I'm so happy to see a new generation of bartenders fall in love with this drink and see them refining their skills to champion one of my all-time favorites."

CLASSIC DRY GREY GOOSE MARTINI

LE MARTINI
GROUND FLOOR, CROWN MELBOURNE, SOUTHBANK

To truly enjoy the classic Martini, here are national brand ambassador for Grey Goose, Corina Retter's, top tips: 1) Use the finest quality ingredients—given the Martini relies on just two ingredients, using quality ingredients is a must; 2) a Martini must be served ice cold to ensure the most enjoyable serve, so always chill your glassware. In addition, a Martini should contain no more than twelve sips to ensure that it stays cold throughout drinking; 3) while some notable pop culture examples may have preferred theirs shaken, not stirred, Corina begs to differ. If you shake a Martini cocktail, it can produce ice chips in an otherwise crystal-clear cocktail and it can add up to 10% more water. She suggests stirring a Martini cocktail gently.

GLASSWARE: Martini glass

GARNISH: Lemon twist

- 1¾ oz. | 50 ml Grey Goose Vodka
- ⅓ oz. | 10 ml Noilly Prat Original Dry Vermouth
- Dash orange bitters

1. Chill a martini glass. Combine all of the ingredients in a mixing glass filled with ice and stir deliberately.
2. Strain the cocktail into the chilled martini glass.
3. Garnish with a lemon twist.

DALE DEGROFF, LE MARTINI

Le Martini showcases a star-studded roster of internationally renowned bartenders curating bespoke cocktail menus, with award-
winning bartending icon Dale DeGroff paying a visit to develop the inaugural cocktail list for the bar. Known for transforming cocktail culture in the 1980s while working at New York's legendary Rainbow
Room, DeGroff says Melbourne is at the forefront of global cocktail
culture. "Melbourne is the perfect location to open Grey Goose's first
standalone bar given its discerning—and insatiable—appetite for
cocktails and, in particular, the Martini," he says. "The city has no
shortage of excellent drinking establishments, so it was meant to be."

DeGroff curated three exclusive Martinis for guests to sip at
Le Martini.

"I wanted to show the evolution of the Martini—from what was
served in 1888 to the nineteenth and twentieth centuries and paying
tribute to the new millennium, and so we've made that happen, all
using the exquisite Grey Goose Vodka, which has been my go-to
vodka since I participated in the world release in New York City
in 1997."

As for DeGroff's personal favorite Martini recipe, he likes his
fifty-fifty—equal parts vodka and vermouth. "I used to drink my Martinis for the power, now I find wetter is better," he says.

GREY GOOSE MARTINIÉ SPECIALE

LE MARTINI
GROUND FLOOR, CROWN MELBOURNE, SOUTHBANK

Bartending legend Dale DeGroff created the opulent Grey Goose Martinié Speciale to celebrate French spirits and wine. DeGroff says Martini appreciation has been taken to new heights in recent years by the expansion of the vermouth category, with many new bottlings and increasingly elevated quality, as well as bar staff having more knowledge and education around using wine-based products.

GLASSWARE: Martini glass

GARNISH: Bono Castelvetrano Whole Sicilian Green Olives

- 2 oz. | 60 ml Grey Goose Vodka
- ½ oz. | 15 ml sauternes
- ½ oz. | 15 ml Dolin Blanc Vermouth
- Dash The Bitter Truth Orange Bitters
- Dash saline solution

1. Chill a martini glass. Combine all of the ingredients in a mixing glass filled with ice and stir to chill and dilute.
2. Strain the cocktail into the chilled martini glass.
3. Garnish with the olives.

HARRY'S ORIGINAL

LE MARTINI
GROUND FLOOR, CROWN MELBOURNE, SOUTHBANK

Dale DeGroff was inspired by the classic 1888 Harry Johnson Martini recipe when creating Harry's Original. "It was the first recipe in print, a five-ingredient version by the way, and equal parts gin and vermouth," he says. "I wanted to pay tribute to that and use vodka and vermouth in this case."

GLASSWARE: Martini glass

- 2 oz. | 60 ml Grey Goose Vodka
- ½ oz. | 15 ml Cocchi Storico Vermouth di Torino
- ½ oz. | 15 ml Noilly Prat Original Dry Vermouth
- 2 dashes gum syrup
- 2 dashes Pierre Ferrand Dry Curaçao
- Dash The Bitter Truth Bogart's Bitters
- 1 lemon zest coin, to express

1. Chill a martini glass. Combine all of the ingredients, except for the lemon coin, in a mixing glass with cracked ice and stir to chill and dilute.

2. Mist the inside of the chilled glass with the oil from a lemon zest coin, discarding the coin, just before straining the drink into the glass.

GREY GOOSE MILLENNIUM DRY MARTINI

LE MARTINI
GROUND FLOOR, CROWN MELBOURNE, SOUTHBANK

Dale DeGroff's Grey Goose Millennium Dry features a crisp profile that pays tribute to the new millennium. "In the United States and Europe, we're seeing an uptick in both gin and vodka Martinis in the luxury market," he says. And this take is certainly luxe. You'll need a kitchen scale to make this recipe properly.

GLASSWARE: Martini glass

GARNISH: Bono Castelvetrano Whole Sicilian Green Olive

- 2 oz. | 60 ml Grey Goose Vodka
- 12.5 grams Noilly Prat Original Dry Vermouth
- 6 grams Dolin Blanc Vermouth
- Dash saline solution
- Dash Dale DeGroff Pimento Aromatic bitters

1. Chill a martini glass. Combine all of the ingredients in a mixing glass filled with ice and stir to chill and dilute.
2. Strain the cocktail into the chilled martini glass.
3. Garnish with the olive.

ANDY CHU, ONE OR TWO

One or Two is located in the heart of Melbourne's Chinatown and is owned by Andy Chu. Born in Australia and raised in Hong Kong, Andy has travelled extensively, shaking the cans in Canada, London, and Scotland, where he developed a passion for whiskey. When he returned to Australia, Andy worked at an impressive roster of Melbourne bars, including BYRDI, The Everleigh, Black Pearl, and Above Board before opening his own "contemporary hideout."

One or Two follows the idea of *wabi-sabi*, a way of living that embraces the imperfect and impermanent. "That could apply to our decorations, drinks, service, or styles," he says. The bar has just twenty-four seats, ten cocktails on the list, sixty whiskies on the backbar, just three wines, two beers, and zero off-menu cocktails. "To keep it simple but also essential," Andy explains.

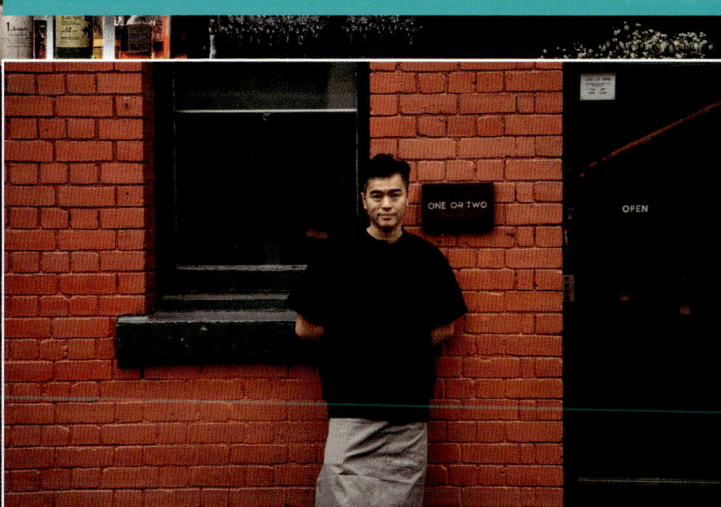

BLUEBERRY YOGHURT PUNCH

ONE OR TWO
18 CELESTIAL AVENUE

According to owner Andy Chu, customers love the Blueberry Yoghurt Punch cocktail because it's fun. "Just think about turning a gelato into a clean cocktail," he says. Andy's recipe makes enough cocktails to satisfy a whole crowd of gelato-flavored-cocktail fans.

GLASSWARE: Rocks glass

GARNISH: Flower

- 16 oz. | 500 ml Roku Gin
- 6¾ oz. | 200 ml G.E. Massenez Crème de Myrtille
- 3½ oz. | 100 ml St-Germain Elderflower Liqueur
- 1¾ oz. | 50 ml Ojo de Tigre Mezcal
- 32 oz. | 1,000 ml blueberry juice
- 2⅓ oz. | 70 ml fresh lemon juice
- 32 oz. | 1,000 ml yogurt

1. In a large container, combine all of the ingredients, except for the yogurt. Pour the yogurt into a separate large container.
2. Pour the mixture into the yogurt and stir. Then place the mixture in the refrigerator for 6 to 24 hours.
3. Place a cheesecloth over a container or jar with a funnel and slowly strain the mixture.
4. Strain the punch again through a coffee filter then place it back in the refrigerator to chill.
5. To serve, pour the punch into a rocks glass over a block of cube ice.
6. Garnish with a flower.

ONE OR TWO OLD FASHIONED

ONE OR TWO
18 CELESTIAL AVE

One or Two owner Andy Chu created the One or Two Old Fashioned as part of a Fourth of July cocktail collaboration with the Distilled Spirits Council of the United States. Twenty-three of the country's finest bartenders and mixologists created cocktails for the Cheers! Spirits from the USA campaign, which aimed to elevate appreciation of American whiskey in Australia. You'll need a kitchen scale to make the syrup properly.

GLASSWARE: Rocks glass

GARNISH: Orange twist

- 1 oz. | 30 ml Angel's Envy Kentucky Straight Bourbon
- 1 teaspoon | 5 ml Brown Syrup (see recipe)
- 2 dashes aromatic bitters
- Dash saline solution
- Dash orange bitters

1. Combine all of the ingredients in a mixing glass with ice and stir for an optimum temperature and dilution.
2. Strain the cocktail over a block of ice.
3. Garnish with an orange twist.

BROWN SYRUP: Using a Thermomix multicooker, or simmering in a saucepan, combine 300 grams superfine (caster) sugar, 15 grams coconut brown sugar, and 150 grams filtered water until the sugar is dissolved. Let the syrup cool.

AMBASSADOR

THE ELYSIAN WHISKY BAR
113 BRUNSWICK STREET, FITZROY

The Elysian Whisky Bar is small and cozy and renowned for its ever-changing backbar of three hundred and fifty bottles of rare and interesting whiskies, with a focus on independent bottlings from around the world. Founder Yao Wong says the Ambassador is a great alternative to a Manhattan as a nightcap cocktail. "While being a richer, booze-forward cocktail, it veers to the lower ABV end of the spectrum, which is quite trendy at the moment," he says. "Make sure the mixing glass and coupette are thoroughly chilled before assembling the cocktail. Use good quality ice if you can, and always ensure your vermouths are as fresh as can be!"

GLASSWARE: Coupette glass

GARNISH: Lemon twist

- 1 oz. | 30 ml Michter's US★1 Kentucky Straight Rye
- ⅔ oz. | 20 ml sweet vermouth
- ⅔ oz. | 20 ml dry vermouth
- 1 teaspoon | 5 ml maraschino liqueur
- 2 dashes orange bitters

1. Chill a coupette. Combine all of the ingredients in a mixing glass with ice and stir.
2. Strain the cocktail into the chilled coupette.
3. Garnish with a lemon twist.

THIRD TIME'S THE CHARM

THE ELYSIAN WHISKY BAR
113 BRUNSWICK STREET, FITZROY

Yao Wong created Third Time's the Charm as part of a Fourth of July cocktail collaboration with the Distilled Spirits Council of the United States (DISCUS). DISCUS is on a mission to raise the profile of American spirits in Australia and joined with twenty-three of Australia's finest bartenders and mixologists on the Cheers! Spirits from the USA campaign.

GLASSWARE: Rocks glass
GARNISH: Orange twist

- ½ oz. | 15 ml Angel's Envy Kentucky Straight Bourbon
- ½ oz. | 15 ml cognac
- 1 teaspoon | 5 ml Pedro Ximénez
- Dash Angostura bitters
- Dash orange bitters

1. Combine all of the ingredients in a mixing glass with ice and stir.
2. Strain the cocktail into a rocks glass over a large rock of ice.
3. Garnish with an orange twist.

1951 CHICAGO MARTINI

GIN PALACE
10 RUSSELL PLACE

Established in 1997, Gin Palace is a Melbourne institution. It was one of the city's original laneway bars and the first to offer table service. Late founder Vernon Chalker's vision for the bar was "a lounge bar opened in Budapest in the 1870s and renovated in the 1950s." Nowadays, says venue manager Nathaniel Stove, "customers love that we don't just serve drinks; we serve an experience." Stove describes what makes Gin Palace work: "Our signatures are our selection of gins, of course—around three hundred and counting—our very long Martinis, our famous toasted chicken sandwiches, and the fact we're open every day from 4 p.m. until 3 a.m. without fail." The 1951 Chicago Martini was one of Vernon's favorite Martinis. "The subtle bitterness of the dry white vermouth balances perfectly with the sweet orange of the Cointreau, and the anchovy-stuffed olives give it an umami kick," Nathan says.

GLASSWARE: Martini glass
GARNISH: Anchovy-stuffed olives

- 3 oz. | 85 ml Sipsmith London Dry Gin
- 1 teaspoon | 5 ml Noilly Prat Original Dry Vermouth
- Cointreau, to spray

1. Chill a martini glass. Pour the gin and vermouth into a mixing glass.
2. Spray the chilled glass with Cointreau.
3. Fill the mixing glass with ice and stir.
4. Strain the cocktail into the martini glass and garnish with the stuffed olives.

MONK REVIVER

Bar Ampere specialises in vermouths, amaros, and absinthes. Sitting atop a vintage electrical substation, its decor is inspired by the classic aperitif bars of Paris. "We serve absinthe the traditional way, with an iced water fountain, absinthe spoons, and sugar cubes so guests can dilute and sweeten their absinthe to their own taste," says venue manager Ryan Jackson. Many of Melbourne's bar managers, bartenders, waiters, and chefs head to the bar after their shifts, as it serves food until 3 a.m. every night of the week. The Monk Reviver is a twist on the classic Corpse Reviver #2, which was designed to "bring one back to life" and features Green Chartreuse. "Bartenders love Chartreuse because it's steeped in history and made by the Carthusian monks of France with a secret recipe featuring one hundred and fifty herbs, plants, and flowers." This cocktail is "strong, complex, and full of flavor, but very easy to drink."

GLASSWARE: Nick & Nora glass

GARNISH: 2 sprays of absinthe, maraschino cherry

- 1⅓ oz. | 40 ml Green Chartreuse
- ⅔ oz. | 20 ml fresh lime juice
- ⅓ oz. | 10 ml simple syrup
- Dash Élixir Végétal de la Grande-Chartreuse

1. Combine all of the ingredients, except for the absinthe, in a cocktail shaker with ice and shake.

2. Double-strain the cocktail into a Nick & Nora.

3. Garnish with 2 sprays of absinthe and a maraschino cherry.

BIJOU

BIJOU BOTTLE STORE
194 LITTLE COLLINS STREET

Bijou seats only twenty-five people but has a huge array of exceptional and rare wines and liquors. There is no menu; instead the staff chat through the daily offerings with each table to ensure that patrons are sipping something that suits their palate and mood. "The bar's name was inspired in a few ways, one being the historic Bijou Theatre in Melbourne in the 1800s, another because it means 'small jewel,'" venue manager Kelsey Stringer says. The bijou cocktail also uses spirits that echo gems—gin (diamond), Green Chartreuse (emerald), and sweet red vermouth (ruby). "Due to our limited space, we serve only the best stirred-down classics here, and the bijou is complex, full flavored, and versatile—we play around with whichever gins and vermouths we're ranging at the time."

GLASSWARE: Nick & Nora glass

GARNISH: Lemon zest

- 1 oz. | 30 ml Green Chartreuse
- 1 oz. | 30 ml gin
- 1 oz. | 30 ml Maidenii Sweet Vermouth

1. Chill a Nick & Nora glass. Combine all of the ingredients in a mixing glass. Fill the mixing glass with ice and stir until the outside starts to show condensation.

2. Strain the cocktail through a julep strainer into the chilled Nick & Nora.

3. Garnish with a lemon zest.

BANK OF TIME

Black Kite Commune is inspired by the supper clubs of Melbourne in the 1900s—moody, boisterous, and serving liquor and food until late into the night. The striking decor includes a golden-tiled backbar and a huge backlit photograph of the night sky on the ceiling. "There are so many vantage points in this space; you can be front row to the bar or hidden away upstairs making use of our service buttons from the loft booths," says venue manager Jess Clayfield. "We're known for our curated selection of Australian liquors, and Bank of Time combines a few of our favourites, while also featuring our house-made cola." For the latter, you can substitute with any craft cola.

GLASSWARE: Martini glass

GARNISH: Brandy-soaked cherry

- 1½ oz. | 45 ml Archie Rose Double Malt Whisky

- ½ oz. | 15 ml Scarlet Sweet Vermouth

- ¼ oz. | 7.5 ml Dasher + Fisher Cherry Gin

- ½ oz. | 15 ml Black Kite Commune Native Cola

1. Combine all of the ingredients in a mixing glass. Fill the mixing glass with ice and stir until the outside starts to show condensation.

2. Strain the cocktail into a martini glass and garnish with a brandy-soaked cherry.

JOHNNY PASH

LULIE TAVERN
225 JOHNSTON STREET, ABBOTSFORD

Stepping inside Lulie takes you miles away from the hustle and bustle of the busy streets outside and into a dimly lit bar that you might find on a neighbourhood corner anywhere in the world. "The feel of the place is worn in and about as comfortable as it gets," says owner Brendan Kennedy. The bar's Johnny Pash cocktail is "a zesty kiss on the lips, and a little reminiscent of the Australian favorite Frosty Fruits, a type of popsicle," Brendan adds.

GLASSWARE: Coupe glass

GARNISH: Dehydrated lime wheel

- 1 oz. | 30 ml gin
- 1 oz. | 30 ml passion fruit puree
- ½ oz. | 15 ml Mathilde Poire
- ½ oz. | 15 ml fresh lemon juice

1. Combine all of the ingredients in a Boston shaker with ice and shake vigorously.
2. Double-strain the cocktail into a coupe and garnish with a dehydrated lime wheel.

B.A.B

Bouvardia's operations manager Jack Tennant says the B.A.B is a favorite with patrons because it features the perfect balance of sweetness and complexity. "Whether you prefer something on the boozier side when it comes to cocktails, or you want a drink to satiate that sweet tooth, the B.A.B will hit that mark," he says. "The idea came in a few parts from the blackened apples in *The Noma Guide to Fermentation.* The first part was that the blackening process looked like the perfect way to apply unconventional food preparation techniques to drinks. The second part was that brandy often gets a bad rap for being a stuffy, old-timey spirit, and we wanted to try to give it a new lease on life." Tennant added that "the best apples to use are Red Delicious, as they contain slightly more sugar than other varieties, but any decent apples will do in a pinch."

GLASSWARE: Rocks glass

GARNISH: Black apple strips

- • 2 oz. | 60 ml Black Apple Brandy (see recipe)
- • 2 teaspoons | 10 ml Basil Gomme (see recipe)

1. Pour both ingredients into a mixing glass and add ice.
2. Stir the mixture 20 revolutions clockwise, 20 revolutions counterclockwise (this is a rule of thumb to ensure proper dilution).
3. Strain the cocktail into a rocks glass with a large ice rock and garnish with the dehydrated black apple strips.

BLACK APPLE BRANDY: Purchase or gather apples, as needed. With gloves on, carefully peel the skin off of each apple. Place the skinned apples into a vacuum seal bag. Not everyone has a dehydrator, so a rice cooker or slow cooker on the warm setting will also work in a pinch. Fit in as many apples as you can up to about 75% of the bag. Note on the bag what date they went on and will come off. Leave the apples in the dehydrator (or slow cooker or rice cooker) on low for 6 to 8 weeks. Prepare a dehydrator tray with parchment paper. You can also use an oven at a low temperature. Place the blackened apples on the parchment paper and squish to an even layer of about 1 inch (2 to 3 centimeters). Place the apples back in the dehydrator (or oven) for 24 hours. Cut the black apple sheet into thin strips and place them in 1 (750 ml) bottle of St. Agnes Bartender's Cut (or your brandy of choice). Leave the mixture to infuse for 7 to 14 days. Strain the brandy and rebottle it, and reserve the black apple strips for garnishes.

BASIL GOMME: Measure 150 grams sugar into 3½ oz. (100 ml) of boiling water and stir to dissolve, then allow the simple syrup to cool. Weigh out and wash 5 grams fresh basil. Place the basil in a blender with about ½ oz. (15 ml) of the simple syrup. Add the remaining syrup then blend for another minute to ensure it is mixed well. Strain the syrup.

MEZCAL SMOKEY NEGRONI

BAR BAMBI
AC/DC LANE

The owners of Bar Bambi—brothers Nick and Daniel Russian— have taken their inspiration for the bar from all around the world, including Europe and New York. "Customers love that you can either pop in for a quick drink, enjoy Italian share plates for dinner with friends, or stay all night and watch the venue transform into a late-night disco," Nick says. According to Daniel, the Mezcal Smokey Negroni is the perfect New Age take on the classic cocktail, as the smoky flavor adds a new layer of depth to the drink. "If you don't know what to order, we always recommend this," he says.

GLASSWARE: Rocks glass

- 1 oz. | 30 ml Campari
- 1 oz. | 30 ml sweet vermouth
- ½ oz. | 15 ml Patrón El Cielo
- ½ oz. | 15 ml Del Maguey Vida Clásico

1. Combine all of the ingredients in a mixing glass with ice and stir with a swizzle stick until well chilled.
2. Strain the cocktail into a rocks glass over a crystal-clear, hand-cut ice block.

SWEET CHEEKS

SAROS
41 HOMER STREET, MOONEE PONDS

Saros features a wraparound bar that ensures unobstructed views no matter where patrons are seated, be it in the restaurant, at the bar, or outdoors. Bartender Niki Dang says the Sweet Cheeks is a standout on the cocktail menu. "It starts with a refreshing burst of tart sourness and high acidity, then seamlessly transitions to a sweet, juniper-driven finish with a smooth, lingering mouthfeel," she says. "This playful balance is truly addictive, and with a cheeky name to match, it's an absolute hit among our guests." To ensure the perfect result, Niki suggests shaking the cocktail for as long as possible, until you feel the shaker start to get icy cold in your hands. This ensures the foam is consistent throughout your drink journey and allows for a smooth sip from start to finish. "Using a more intense gin such as navy strength complements the tart and bold flavors of the Davidson plum well; it brings a peppery and zesty component without over-shining the native fruit," says Dang.

GLASSWARE: Rocks glass
GARNISH: Freeze-fried Davidson plum crumbs,
dehydrated apple wheel, rosemary

- 1 oz. | 30 ml Davidson Plum Syrup (see recipe)
- 1½ oz. | 45 ml navy strength gin
- ⅔ oz. | 20 ml fresh lemon juice
- Wonderfoam Cocktail Foamer, as needed

1. Combine all of the ingredients in a cocktail shaker with ice and shake vigorously.
2. Double-strain the cocktail into a clean shaker and dry-shake (without ice).
3. Strain once more over ice into a rocks glass.
4. Garnish with freeze-fried Davidson plum crumbs, a dehydrated apple wheel, and a sprig of fresh rosemary.

DAVIDSON PLUM SYRUP: Pit and halve 3 Davidson plums, keeping the skin on. Boil the plums with ¼ cup sugar, ¼ cup water, the juice of 1 lemon, and 1 roasted vanilla bean in a pot until the consistency becomes thicker. Strain the syrup and allow it to cool completely before refrigerating for a thick syrup consistency.

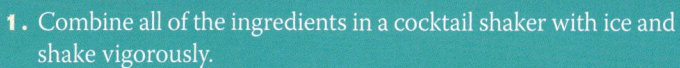

BIERE 75

Brewmanity opened Melbourne's first rooftop brewery bar in early 2024, with a terrace offering expansive city views. Bar manager Sam Edwards loves that the bar is experimenting with beer-based cocktails. Melbourne has a thriving craft beer scene and the Biere 75 is made with beer brewed in the heart of Melbourne. "Biere 75 is a simple and elegant drink—a classic French 75 with a beer twist that's perfect for beer and cocktail lovers alike," he says. If you can't get your hands on Brewmanity Hazy IPA, substitute with a hazy IPA from one of your local craft brewers.

GLASSWARE: Champagne flute

- 1 oz. | 30 ml Tanqueray Sevilla Orange
- ½ oz. | 15 ml fresh lemon juice
- ½ oz. | 15 ml simple syrup
- Brewmanity Hazy IPA, to top

1. Combine all of the ingredients, except for the beer, in a cocktail shaker with ice and shake.
2. Double-strain the cocktail into a champagne flute.
3. Top with the beer.

ROY MARTINS DAS NEVES, BEVERLY ROOFTOP

Sitting above the hustle and bustle of Chapel Street, Beverly Rooftop is as sophisticated as she is relaxed. A visit to the bar provides breathtaking views—270 degrees, in fact—of the Melbourne cityscape.

Bar manager Roy Martins Das Neves says the Beverly Rooftop is known for its dedication to sustainable and ethical practices, with a focus on mitigating waste and repurposing both the bar and as much as much of the kitchen's leftover ingredients as possible. "Our sustainable ethos doesn't stop with cocktails, but rather transcends through to the entire beverage offering," he says. "We align ourselves with brands that share the same ethos, brands that cut against the grain to do something different for the environment while adhering to ethical practices."

Beverly's drinks list has been curated to highlight locally sourced products, ranging from craft beers to its selection of Australian wines and spirits. On the cocktail list, familiar classics are given new life with native herbs, locally made spirits, and unique garnishes.

GOLDEN GIRL

BEVERLY ROOFTOP
LEVEL 24/627 CHAPEL STREET, SOUTH YARRA

The Golden Girl is a delicious low-ABV cocktail, with sweet and tart profiles, along with herbal notes. "Thanks to the orange cream citrate and lactic acid, it gives off a creamy sherbet feel with a dryness that will leave you salivating for more," says its creator, Roy Martins Das Neves. The cocktail also highlights apricots, which nods to Victoria being the biggest producer of the fruit in Australia. "We Melburnians love our stone fruit, especially apricots," Das Neves says. While Das Neves ferments apricots and mixes them with apricot syrup, apricot juice can serve as a simpler at-home alternative.

GLASSWARE: Nick & Nora glass

GARNISH: Agrumato oil

- 1½ oz. | 45 ml Unico Pomelo Dry White Vermouth
- 17/20 oz. | 25 ml apricot juice
- 3½ teaspoons | 17.5 ml Lactic Acid Solution (see recipe)
- ½ oz. | 15 ml fresh lemon juice
- 1 teaspoon | 5 ml absinthe
- 3 dashes | 2 ml Bittermens Orange Cream Bitters

1. Chill a Nick & Nora glass. Combine all of the ingredients in a mixing glass and stir.

2. Pre-batch the mixture with a 10% water dilution (⅓ oz. water) then chill the batch in the refrigerator.

3. To serve, pour the cocktail into the chilled Nick & Nora.

4. Garnish with Agrumato oil.

LACTIC ACID SOLUTION: In a container, combine 5 grams lactic acid (it usually comes as a 70% solution) with 100 grams (100 ml) water. Stir to blend and bottle the solution.

SUMMER OF '95

Located in the heart of Melbourne's entertainment and political district, Punch Lane has been an institution in Melbourne for almost thirty years. "A lot of our customers have some preconceptions about wine, and the team at Punch Lane really try hard to break a lot of those walls down, says Nick Gallant, bar manager. "Adding red wine to this cocktail pays homage to just how versatile wine can be. It also looks very good if layered properly. I like to put a nip pourer into the red wine bottle to control the flow and ensure a clean layer."

GLASSWARE: Nick & Nora glass

- 1 oz. | 30 ml vodka
- 1 oz. | 30 ml fresh lemon juice
- ⅔ oz. | 20 ml Disaronno Originale
- ⅓ oz. | 10 ml cherry liqueur
- 5 drops Bittermens Burlesque Bitters
- 4 drops Wonderfoam Cocktail Foamer
- ⅔ oz. | 20 ml shiraz / syrah, to float

1. Combine all of the ingredients, except for the wine, in a cocktail shaker with ice and shake.
2. Double-strain the cocktail into a Nick & Nora.
3. Hold a barspoon just below the foam and gently layer the red wine float on top.

PORNSTAR MARTINI

Garden State is a lively oasis in the heart of Melbourne's CBD. Venue manager Chanel Von-Lyn describes it as the perfect spot for both after-work drinks and a "late-night cocktail and boogie." Melburnians have embraced the Pornstar Martini in recent years and it has become a firm favorite on the Garden State's cocktail menu. "Like Melbourne, it's always there for a good time," Chanel explains. When it comes to ensuring the perfect serve, Chanel suggests: "Don't be shy with the double strain! A wider fine strainer is recommended for that creamy foamy finish. Delish!"

GLASSWARE: Coupe glass

GARNISH: Passion fruit half

- 1⅓ oz. | 40 ml vanilla vodka
- 1 oz. | 30 ml fresh lemon juice
- 1 oz. | 30 ml passion fruit puree
- ⅔ oz. | 20 ml passion fruit liqueur
- ½ oz. | 15 ml simple syrup
- 1 oz. | 30 ml sparkling wine, to serve

1. Combine all of the ingredients, except for the wine, in a cocktail shaker with ice and shake.
2. Double-strain the cocktail into a coupe.
3. Garnish with half a passion fruit and serve with a shot of sparkling wine.

RITUAL

BENEATH DRIVER LANE
SHOP 3, DRIVER LANE

Melburnians love to uncover hidden gems and Beneath Driver Lane delivers. Tucked away down a laneway and in a basement, it offers live music four nights a week and five hundred whiskies on the backbar. "This is a bar you'd want to end up in if there was an apocalypse," jokes venue manager Kealan Brady. Ritual gives a creative Irish whiskey twist to one of the city's favorite cocktails, the Espresso Martini. The texture produced by the nitrogen in the cocktail gives it the appearance of a settling Guinness. "The deception of others thinking it is a Guinness is a nice trick on the mind, which customers really enjoy," says Kealan. "Just like a good pint of Guinness, make sure to tip the glass when you're pouring the drink and wait until it settles before you take a sip."

GLASSWARE: 8 oz. beer glass
GARNISH: Passion fruit half

- 1½ oz. | 45 ml Bushmills Black Bush Irish Whiskey
- 1 oz. | 30 ml cold brew coffee
- 17/20 oz. | 25 ml water

- ⅓ oz. | 10 ml Amaro di Angostura
- ⅓ oz. | 10 ml Okar Mocha
- ⅓ oz. | 10 ml demerara syrup
- 3 dashes chocolate bitters

180 — MELBOURNE COCKTAILS

1. Combine all of the ingredients in an iSi cream whipper and charge twice with NO₂ cannisters and let the whipper sit for 5 minutes.

2. Pour the cocktail directly from the whipper into a small beer glass.

3. Garnish with a passion fruit half.

TWELFTH NIGHT

JULIET MELBOURNE.
BASEMENT/37-41 LITTLE BOURKE STREET

According to venue manager Benjamin Ogden, the charm of the Twelfth Night lies in the subtle warmth of cinnamon and caraway, which enhance the smoothness of the whiskey. The drink is also elevated by the jammy fruit notes of fresh figs. If figs aren't in season, Ogden recommends keeping the dried figs from the syrup to use as the drink's garnish.

GLASSWARE: Rocks glass

GARNISH: Fig half on a skewer

- 1½ oz. | 45 ml whiskey
- 1 oz. | 30 ml port
- 1 oz. | 30 ml Fig & Cinnamon Syrup (see recipe)
- ½ oz. | 15 ml fresh lemon juice

1. Combine all of the ingredients in a mixing glass with ice and stir down.
2. Strain the cocktail into a rocks glass.
3. Garnish with half a fig skewered on a cocktail skewer.

FIG & CINNAMON SYRUP: In a saucepan over low heat, combine 250 grams dried figs, 250 grams sugar, 300 grams (300 ml, or 9¾ oz.) water, 2 cinnamon sticks, and 3 grams caraway seeds and simmer for 15 minutes. Remove from heat and let the syrup cool. Strain and bottle.

BRISKET MARTINI

FANCY HANK'S
1/79 BOURKE STREET

Fancy Hank's serves up smoked meats out of a two-ton smoker and pairs them with cocktails. "Our Brisket Martini is a unique offering to Fancy Hank's and to Melbourne generally, as it incorporates our famous sixteen-hour smoked brisket into a classic cocktail," says venue manager and cocktail creator Nam Nguyen, who advises that the longer the brisket fat sits in the vodka, the better the cocktail's flavors will be.

GLASSWARE: Martini glass

GARNISH: Olive and beef brisket on a skewer

- 2 oz. | 60 ml Brisket Fat-Washed Vodka (see recipe)
- 1 teaspoon | 5 ml olive brine
- ⅓ oz. | 10 ml Carpano Antica Formula Vermouth

1. Chill a martini glass. Pour the vodka and olive brine into a mixing glass.
2. Line the inside of the chilled martini glass with the vermouth, pouring the remaining liquid into the mixing glass.
3. Add ice to the mixing glass and gently stir down for 45 seconds.
4. Double-strain the cocktail into the martini glass.
5. Garnish with a skewered olive and cubes of brisket.

BRISKET FAT-WASHED VODKA: Decide on your fat source—Fancy Hank's uses the fat from its 16-hour smoked brisket. Render the fat by cooking it in a saucepan over low heat until it becomes liquified. Add the rendered fat to 1 (750 ml) bottle of vodka then chill the vodka in the freezer for at least 4 to 5 hours, longer if you have time. The fat will solidify on top of the alcohol, making it easier to remove. Strain the vodka through a cheesecloth or coffee filter.

MELBOURNE MADE

Good Heavens is Melbourne's largest rooftop bar, serving up colorful cocktails, craft beers, and an extensive wine list in the heart of the city. The Melbourne Made is named in honor of the local spirits it contains: Melbourne Moonshine Apple Pie and Gospel Solera Rye. "Melbourne Made hits all the flavors in one combination—sour, sweet, and tropical," says bar manager Alex Robertson.

GLASSWARE: Coupe glass

GARNISH: 3 drops Angostura bitters

- 1 oz. | 30 ml Melbourne Moonshine Apple Pie Shine
- 1 oz. | 30 ml The Gospel Solera Rye
- 1 oz. | 30 ml pineapple juice
- 1 oz. | 30 ml fresh lemon juice
- ½ oz. | 15 ml simple syrup

1. Chill a coupe glass. Combine all of the ingredients in a cocktail shaker with ice and hard-shake for 10 to 12 seconds.
2. Double-strain the cocktail into the chilled coupe.
3. Garnish with 3 drops of Angostura bitters, and draw lines in the dots.

FLAMING FOX

MAEVE FOX
472 CHURCH STREET, CREMORNE

The Flaming Fox is served with captivating showmanship and Instagram-worthy flames. It immediately commands attention and creates an unforgettable spectacle. Beyond the flair, the cocktail surprises with its easy-drinking nature, balanced flavors, and smooth finish.

GLASSWARE: Collins glass

GARNISH: Passion fruit half, sugar cube soaked in bitters, orange oil

- 1 oz. | 30 ml Wyborowa Vodka
- ½ oz. | 15 ml Absolut Vanilia Vodka
- ½ oz. | 15 ml Villa Massa Limoncello
- 1 teaspoon | 5 ml Vok Parfait Amour Liqueur
- ⅓ oz. | 10 ml Monin Passion Fruit Syrup
- Orange juice, to top
- Passion fruit juice, to top

1. Combine all of the ingredients, except for the juices, in a cocktail shaker with ice and shake.
2. Strain the cocktail over ice into a collins glass.
3. Garnish with half of a passion fruit with a sugar cube soaked in bitters. Then light the sugar cube on fire, and spray it with two sprays of orange oil.

MARITIME SOUR

Renowned chef and restaurateur Luke Mangan recently opened his first Melbourne restaurant in more than a decade, Bistrot Bisou. Located in the Hotel Indigo, the relaxed French bistro and bar features modern takes on classic French dishes and cocktails, together with a sharp wine list. Mangan was born in Melbourne and says it is exciting to be back in the city because it has a European feel to it, especially during the cooler months. "We want Bistrot Bisou to feel like a second home for guests, whether they're Melbourne locals or visitors wanting a relaxed place to dine after a long day of sightseeing," he says. Restaurant and bar manager Tim Davey says the Maritime Sour is the perfect aperitif. "It is balanced, fresh, and clean. It cleanses your palate, not unlike a sorbet," he says.

GLASSWARE: Coupe glass

GARNISH: Lemon peel

- 2 oz. | 60 ml Bass & Flinders Maritime Gin
- 1 oz. | 30 ml fresh lemon juice
- ½ oz. | 15 ml orgeat
- 4 shakes of Fee Brothers Fee Foam

1. Combine all of the ingredients in a cocktail shaker with ice and shake.
2. Double-strain the cocktail into a coupe.
3. Garnish with a strip of lemon peel.

SALTBUSH MARGARITA

FOSSEY'S DISTILLERY
209 LYGON STREET, CARLTON

The upstairs cocktail bar at Fossey's Distillery is a cozy haunt, and this Margarita is a frequent request. "Customers love the saltiness of the gin and the tartness of the lemon and lime juice, not to forget the gin salt around the glass," says venue manager Natasha Beckman. Fossey's makes its own commercially available gin salt, featuring Murray River pink salt and gin botanicals. However, a pink salt rim is a suitable alternative for cocktail enthusiasts who are unable to source a jar of Fossey's.

GLASSWARE: Nick & Nora glass

GARNISH: Lime wheel

- Fossey's Gin Salt, for the rim
- 2 oz. | 60 ml Fossey's Old Man Saltbush Gin
- ½ oz. | 15 ml fresh lemon juice
- 2 teaspoons | 10 ml fresh lime juice
- 2 teaspoons | 10 ml orange curaçao

1. Wet the rim of a Nick & Nora then dip the glass rim into the salt.
2. Combine the remaining ingredients in a cocktail shaker with ice and shake.
3. Fine-strain the cocktail into the rimmed Nick & Nora.
4. Garnish with a lime wheel.

FLAMINGO SOURS

BLACKSMITH BAR & GRILL
VOCO MELBOURNE CENTRAL, LEVEL 7,
30 TIMOTHY LANE

Blacksmith Bar & Grill is an atmospheric venue featuring striking Gothic arches, an angelic centerpiece above the bar, and panoramic views of the skyline, which are breathtaking at sunset. The Flamingo Sours was originally crafted by general manager Celeste Clarke, who opened the voco Melbourne Central hotel, and it has since been reimagined by head mixologist Sam Osborne. "Guests often ask, 'What's that cocktail you just served?'" Osborne says. "The Raspberry & Thyme Shrub makes our Flamingo Sours stand out from the classic Clover Club we used to inspire our twist. It's really in your face with its vibrant color." He adds that it all comes down to the shake. "Dry- and wet-shaking is essential with Sour-style cocktails," he explains. "Dry-shaking helps emulsify the egg whites—or plant-based substitute—with the rest of the ingredients. This gives it that fluffy, glossy finish."

GLASSWARE: Coupe glass

GARNISH: Raspberries on a skewer

- 2 oz. | 60 ml Gallivanter Gin
- ⅔ oz. | 20 ml fresh lemon juice
- 1 oz. | 30 ml Raspberry & Thyme Shrub (see recipe)
- ⅔ oz. | 20 ml egg white or aquafaba

1. Chill a coupe glass. Combine all of the ingredients in a cocktail shaker and dry-shake (without ice).

2. Add ice then wet-shake.

3. Double-strain the cocktail into the chilled coupe.

4. Garnish with raspberries on a skewer.

RASPBERRY & THYME SHRUB: In a sterilized large jar, combine 2 cups fresh raspberries, 1 cup sugar, 2 cups apple cider vinegar, and 8 sprigs fresh thyme and seal the jar. Allow the mixture to ferment for at least 5 days in the refrigerator. Use a fine-mesh strainer lined with cheesecloth to strain out the solids, pressing with a wooden spoon, so the shrub runs into a clean jar.

PLEASE DON'T TELL COLADA

STEAK MINISTRY
39 KINGSWAY PARADE, GLEN WAVERLEY

Steak Ministry matches an extensive range of Asian-influenced spirits with premium Australian steaks. The venue's Please Don't Tell Colada highlights Tanduay Especia Spiced Rum from the Philippines, which bar manager Ashan Welhenage describes as the best spiced rum on the market. "The cocktail is tropical, bubbly, and bursting with flavor," he says.

GLASSWARE: Collins glass

GARNISH: Tropical flower, pineapple leaf

- 1⅓ oz. | 40 ml Tanduay Especia Spiced Rum
- ⅔ oz. | 20 ml Malibu
- ⅔ oz. | 20 ml coconut puree
- 1 oz. | 30 ml pineapple juice
- 1 teaspoon | 5 ml fresh lime juice
- 1 teaspoon | 5 ml simple syrup
- 2⅓ oz. | 70 ml Coconut Soda Foam (see recipe), to top
- Soda water, to top

1. Combine all of the ingredients, except for the soda foam and soda water, in a cocktail shaker with ice and shake.
2. Double-strain the cocktail into a collins glass.
3. Top with the soda foam and soda water.
4. Garnish with a tropical flower and a pineapple leaf.

COCONUT SODA FOAM: Add ½ cup coconut milk, ½ oz. lime juice, and 1 tablespoon simple syrup to a cream whipper. Shake, charge, shake, and dispense.

HOUSE SPRITZ

EMBLA
122 RUSSELL STREET

Wine is the focus at Embla, but the bar staff mixes a few classics, mainly Martinis, Spritzes, Old Fashioneds, and Negronis. The House Spritz features a vermouth, created by the bar's co-owner and chef, Dave Verheul, made from fourteen different flowers that have been wild picked or grown organically. They include marigolds, rose geranium, elderflowers, and chamomile, which are blended into a moscato base wine. If you can't get your hands on a bottle, substitute a floral-infused craft vermouth.

GLASSWARE: Wineglass

GARNISH: Lemon verbena oil, lemon twist

- 1½ oz. | 45 ml Saison Aperitifs Summer Flowers Vermouth
- 2 oz. | 60 ml prosecco
- Splash of soda, to top

1. In the order of ingredients listed, build the cocktail over ice in a wineglass.
2. Garnish with lemon verbena oil and a lemon twist.

RUSSELL BRANFORD, ARLECHIN

Melbourne hospitality legends the Grossi family recently reopened their European-style bar Arlechin, which features a cocktail list by bar manager Russell Branford. Branford was formerly at renowned regional Victorian restaurant Lake House, which has been drawing foodies to the town of Daylesford for more than forty years. Behind the bar at Arlechin, Branford makes his cocktails with a premium selection of ingredients that are infused in-house.

Expect to find signature cocktails such as the Puttanesca Martinez, a take on the classic pasta sauce, and A Little Bit of Fancy, a reimagining of the classic champagne cocktail with the addition of a Campari-soaked sugar cube dropped into the glass tableside to create a fizzing spectacle. The drinks menu also features a selection of classics with a twist, including a barrel-aged Grossi Negroni, Bellini, Paloma, and more.

For those wanting expert advice or a classic that's off the menu, Branford says his team is equipped to make almost anything. "What I love most about hospitality is the unique way we bond with our team and the special interactions we have with our guests," he says. "There aren't many things better than going out, having a good time, and feeling as though you are truly looked after."

PUTTANESCA MARTINEZ

Arlechin resembles an old European wine cellar with its curved cork roof. The venue's subterranean ambience invites guests to step inside and immerse themselves in the intimate space. The Puttanesca Martinez, inspired by the classic Martinez, incorporates flavors from the Italian pasta sauce, puttanesca. It was inspired by the discovery of a mural outside the entry of Arlechin depicting the sauce. "For me, it's all about the science and special processes that enhance the appearance and texture of a cocktail whilst maintaining its flavor profile," venue manager Russell Branford says. "For instance, we make tomato oil in-house for our Puttanesca Martinez. This involves semi-dehydrating tomatoes until they have a leather texture, then blitzing them with a bit of heat and straining the juice out so you're left with this beautiful aromatic flavor." Arlechin's recipes for tomato oil and black olive reduction are closely guarded by the kitchen, but here are ways to make your own.

GLASSWARE: Martini glass
GARNISH: 1 basil leaf, 5 drops Tomato-Infused Oil (see recipe)

- 1½ oz. | 45 ml Chile-Infused Gin (see recipe)
- 1 oz. | 30 ml 1757 Vermouth di Torino G.I. Rosso

- Barspoon caper brine
- 1 pipette Black Olive Reduction (see recipe)
- 5 drops hellfire bitters

1. Combine all of the ingredients in a mixing glass with ice.
2. Stir down the mixture until perfectly chilled and subtly diluted, then strain the cocktail into a martini glass.
3. To garnish, fold the basil leaf in half and cut a diagonal incision so it can slot onto the edge of your glass.
4. Garnish with 5 drops of tomato oil spaced evenly over the surface of the cocktail.

CHILE-INFUSED GIN: Add 2 birds eye chile peppers, chopped, to 1 (750 ml) bottle of gin. Allow the mixture to infuse for at least for 24 hours.

TOMATO-INFUSED OIL: Roast a container of grape tomatoes and add them to a food processor with 1 cup olive oil. Allow the oil to infuse for 30 minutes. Puree the mixture then allow it to infuse for another 30 minutes. Strain the oil through a cheesecloth-lined strainer over a medium bowl, discarding the tomatoes.

BLACK OLIVE REDUCTION:
In a saucepan over medium-low heat, combine 10 oz. sugar and 3 tablespoons water and simmer, stirring, until the mixture is light golden in color. Puree 10 oz. pitted black olives in a food processor then pass the puree through a cheesecloth-lined strainer over a medium bowl. Add the olive puree to the saucepan and stir well to combine. Remove the reduction from heat and let it cool.

TOM HOPE, COMMIS

Bar manager Tom Hope says the appeal of Commis is that it "feels like coming home. The overwhelming feedback we have had since the day we opened is that it feels like it's always been here. The offerings are complex and well balanced, but the vibe is relaxed. When you walk into the space it's like a big warm hug."

The venue is also filled with art—the walls feature an ever-changing selection for patrons to both view and buy. It's a soul-filling environment for Tom, who is an artist by day and bartender by night—you may catch him sketching between mixing drinks!

CHARLIE GREY

Bar manager Tom Hope says the Charlie Grey is a favorite with customers because it balances the "fun and the fruity" and the "balanced and the sophisticated. The cocktail is quintessentially Melbourne, in both in its ingredients and vibe," Hope says. "The spirits are local. And, just like the locals, the drink is always fashionable and sophisticated but never pretentious and has that gritty edge." Hope advises not to over-brew the Earl Grey tea or subject the leaves to active heat, as it will bring too many tannins into the syrup and muddle the prettier flavors of the bergamot. "The trick is making the tea as strong as you can without losing the complexity," he says.

GLASSWARE: Rocks glass

GARNISH: Dehydrated lemon wheel

- **Earl Grey Sugar (see recipe), for the rim**
- **1 oz. | 30 ml MGC Melbourne Dry Gin**
- **1 oz. | 30 ml Marionette Apricot Brandy**
- **1 oz. | 30 ml fresh lemon juice**
- **1 oz. | 30 ml Earl Grey Syrup (see recipe)**

1. Wet the rim of a rocks glass then dip the glass rim in Earl Grey Sugar to give it a rim. Combine the remaining ingredients in a cocktail shaker with ice and shake.

2. Double-strain the cocktail into the rocks glass with a large ice cube.

3. Garnish with a dehydrated lemon wheel.

EARL GREY SYRUP: Steep 10 grams good-quality Earl Grey tea in 3½ oz. (100 ml) boiling water for 30 minutes, then strain and combine with 3½ oz. (100 ml) superfine (caster) sugar. Stir until the sugar is dissolved. Allow the syrup to cool before use.

EARL GREY SUGAR: Grind Earl Grey tea until it's a fine powder, then mix it with white sugar until it reaches a salt-and-pepper appearance.

CAMERON PARISH, GIMLET AT CAVENDISH HOUSE

You will find Gimlet inside a landmark 1920s building. It aims to bring classic European charm a touch of nostalgia with an unmistakably Melbourne style.

Cameron Parish kicked off his hospitality career while he was playing professional football in Manchester, England, and studying physiotherapy. He started working at a bar in the Northern Quarter and loved it so much that he dropped out to work full time as a bartender.

Cameron moved home to Sydney in 2015 and worked as a bartender at the award-wining Bulletin Place. In early 2016 he relocated to Melbourne and worked at one the city's most-loved cocktail bars, The Everleigh, before joining Gimlet in 2019.

Parish has cemented himself as one of the city's best creators and mixers of drinks—his creativity, palate, and encyclopedic knowledge of classic drinks are cornerstones of Gimlet's charm and personality.

GIMLET

Bar manager Cameron Parish says that while the Gimlet is the bar's namesake, it's a favorite with customers for many reasons—gin's juniper fragrance is balanced by gentle sweetness and the brightness of citrus. "It's a thirst quencher through all of Melbourne's highs," he says. Cameron says that the version of the cocktail he has shared is a classic one that can easily be made at home. He suggests using a frozen glass and good ice, then "taste as you go."

GLASSWARE: Coupe glass

GARNISH: Edible white flower

- 1½ oz. | 45 ml Tanqueray London Dry Gin
- ¾ oz. | 22 ml Lime Cordial (see recipe)
- ½ oz. | 15 ml Moscato D'Asti
- 2 pinches salt

1. Chill a coupe glass. Combine all of the ingredients in a mixing glass with ice and stir approximately 10 to 15 times.

2. Strain the cocktail into the chilled coupe.

3. Garnish with a small edible white flower.

LIME CORDIAL: Place the zest of 2 limes, a drop of bergamot oil, and a drop of Geraldton Wax oil with 14 oz. (400 grams) sugar in a jug and mix them together so that everything is evenly distributed. Allow it to sit for 15 minutes, until the oils are infused with sugar. Add 14 oz. (400 ml) verjus and mix until the sugar is dissolved. Strain the cordial through a cheesecloth, coffee filter, or a fine-mesh strainer.

LUCIEN GAUDIN

Apollo Inn is located inside a 1920s neo-renaissance-style building on the corner of Flinders and Hosier Lanes in Melbourne. Taking its cues from the timeless cocktail bars of Europe, Apollo Inn is an ode to the ageless art of the cocktail. Bar manager Cameron Parish says the Lucien Gaudin takes the best elements of two different drinks—the Martini and the Negroni. Named in honor of a French fencer who won gold medals at the 1924 Olympics in Paris, it embodies vintage charm and is the perfect foil for a cold evening. "This drink is suited for making in a big batch ahead of time and serving from the freezer," he says. The recipe below is a variation of the Apollo Inn's Lucien Gaudin, adapted by Cameron for ease of mixing at home. To make it simpler still, substitute Grand Marnier for the house recipe.

GLASSWARE: Nick & Nora glass

- 1 oz. | 30 ml Tanqueray London Dry Gin
- ¾ oz. | 22 ml House Marnier (see recipe)
- ¾ oz. | 22 ml Scarpa Vermouth di Torino Extra Dry
- ½ oz. | 15 ml Campari

1. Chill a Nick & Nora glass. Combine all of the ingredients in a mixing glass with ice and stir approximately 10 to 15 times.
2. Strain the cocktail into the chilled Nick & Nora.

HOUSE MARNIER: Chop 1 lb. (500 grams) blood oranges into quarters and add them to a vacuum bag with 50 grams shio koji and 17 oz. (500 ml) cognac. Let the mixture rest for 24 hours then strain it through a coffee filter. Add 3½ oz. (100 ml) skin-contact orange wine, 3½ oz. (100 ml) 2:1 simple syrup, and 3½ oz. (100 ml) verjus and stir to combine.

LUKE WHEARTY, BYRDI

BYRDI was opened in 2019 by Luke Whearty and co-founder Aki Nishikura, the duo behind Singapore's multi-award-winning—and World's 50 Best Bars regular—Operation Dagger. "BYRDI was born out of a desire to adapt to our environment," Whearty says. "To take culture and cuisine, inspiration and idea, and make it our own. No matter what city we make home."

Tucked into a food precinct called Ella, the bar features its own lab, which is used to create the unique ingredients that are fermented, distilled, and even centrifuged into highly complex, delicious drinks. "We focus purely on local and seasonal produce and exclusively use Australian spirits," Whearty says, adding, "The menu also changes with the seasons to highlight the best produce available at that point in time."

The bar also features bottled cocktails to take home, which offer uniquely Australian twists on the classics, including a Wattleseed Negroni, Waxflower & White Chocolate G&T, and a Paperbark Martini.

FUR & FEATHERS

BYRDI
211 LA TROBE STREET

T he Fur & Feathers cocktail has a unique presentation, served in a small glass bowl inside a handmade feather cup. Co-owner Luke Whearty describes its flavors as "strangely exotic yet local. Make sure your glassware is frozen and the individual elements are all filtered and properly chilled before mixing," he advises. The complex cocktail is created using three separate recipes: Rainforest Eau-de-Vie, Fig Leaf Umeshu, and Shio Koji Honey Water. It also includes unique Austra-lian ingredients such as rainforest cherries, which are described as tasting like "the love child of a watermelon and a cherry."

GLASSWARE: Small glass bowl inside a handmade feather cup

- 1⅓ oz. | 40 ml Rainforest Cherry Eau-de-Vie (see recipe)
- ⅓ oz. | 10 ml Fig Leaf Umeshu (see recipe)

- ⅓ oz. | 10 ml apple, pear, and quince cider
- 1 teaspoon | 5 ml Shio Koji Honey Water (see recipe)

1. Freeze a small glass bowl. Combine all of the ingredients in a mixing glass with ice and stir.

2. Strain the cocktail over a hand-chipped ice sphere into the frozen glass bowl.

3. Place the bowl inside a handmade feather cup.

RAINFOREST CHERRY EAU-DE-VIE: In a Thermomix (or use a blender), blend together 17 oz. (500 ml) apple spirit, 17 oz. (500 ml) plum shochu, 25 grams fresh rainforest cherries, 3½ oz. (100 ml) pomegranate molasses, and 10 grams Davidson plum powder. Place the mixture in a vacuum bag and leave it to infuse at room temperature overnight. Strain the eau-de-vie through a chinois and coffee filter.

FIG LEAF UMESHU: In a vacuum bag, combine 34 oz. (1 liter) sour plum umeshu and 4 large fig leaves. Leave the mixture to rest at room temperature for 48 hours. Strain the umeshu through a chinois and coffee filter.

SHIO KOJI HONEY WATER: Combine 6¾ oz. (200 ml) honey, 6¾ oz. (200 ml) water, 3½ oz. (100 ml) liquid shio koji, and ⅔ oz. (20 ml) vanilla essence and refrigerate until ready to use.

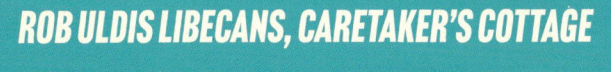

ROB ULDIS LIBECANS, CARETAKER'S COTTAGE

Caretaker's Cottage took the number 23 spot on The World's 50 Best Bars list in 2023. Set in a 107-year-old blue-stone cottage situated behind a church, it is a unique and atmospheric location for a bar.

"We are surrounded by skyscrapers, which creates a little oasis in the city where old meets new," says director and bar manager Rob Uldis Libecans. "We have adopted that with the style of drinks we serve, too."

Uldis Libecans says Caretaker's is fun and warm in all seasons. "We have a diverse clientele, which suggests there's something for everyone here," he says. "We treat the space like a pub, a place that feels comfortable and that doesn't require an explanation. Hopefully it is something that will stand the test of time. We have a deep love for music; it's front and center in every room at the cottage. Vinyl records spin all day every day, played from a handmade set of bronze speakers."

The cocktail menu at Caretaker's Cottage changes every month. "It's a really small space with only thirty seats inside, so we balance a small offering of eight cocktails by rotating often," Uldis Libecans says. "This allows our team to constantly create new drinks and guests to always have something new to try."

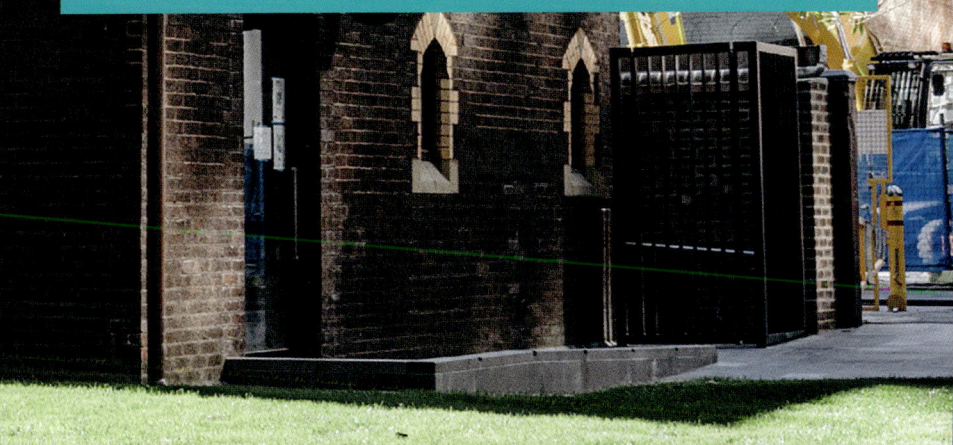

MALTED BALI

Malted Bali is still often requested by guests nearly a year after it left the menu," says Caretaker's Cottage director and bar manager Rob Uldis Libecans. "It's a rich tropical drink that finishes dry with a lot of flavors delicately layered. It's also striking on the eye with its bright green and yellow colors. Whenever we do international guest shifts at bars, we have this on our menu. The wattle is a snapshot in time for the flavor, as the pollen is available for only a short time. The combination of pandan and coconut is so prevalent in Southeast Asian desserts, and those cultures and cuisines are what make Melbourne the food capital of Australia."

GLASSWARE: Porcelain cup

GARNISH: Wattle flowers

- 1½ oz. | 45 ml Coconut & Pandan Syrup (see recipe)
- 1¼ oz. | 35 ml The Balvenie DoubleWood 12
- ½ oz. | 15 ml Wattle Pollen–Infused Sherry (see recipe)
- ½ oz. | 15 ml fresh lemon juice

1. Combine all of the ingredients in a cocktail shaker with ice and shake until cold.
2. Pour the cocktail over a block of ice into a porcelain cup.
3. Garnish with wattle flowers on a stem.

WATTLE POLLEN–INFUSED SHERRY: Infuse 5 grams of wattle pollen in 1 (750 ml) bottle of amontillado sherry. Allow the infusion to rest for 24 hours, then fine-strain and bottle the sherry.

COCONUT & PANDAN SYRUP: In a blender, combine 16½ oz. (500 grams) organic coconut cream, 16½ oz. (500 grams) superfine (caster) sugar, and 3 grams pandan essence and blend until smooth.

TASH CONTE, BLACK PEARL

It has been more than twenty-one years since Black Pearl director Tash Conte convinced her family to leave the restaurant trade and sling cocktails instead. Her staff initially sought inspiration for their creations from a book called *1001 Cocktails*, but it wasn't long before the bar was winning major awards for its libations and world-class service, including being named Best International Cocktail Bar at the 2017 Spirited Awards.

Some of Melbourne's most renowned bartenders have shaken the cans at Black Pearl over the years, including Caretaker's Cottage co-owner Rob Uldis Libecans and three-time winner of the Australian Bartender of the Year title, Chris Hysted-Adams.

"Black Pearl has always been a neighbourhood cocktail bar making the best drinks we can," says Conte. "Although, more importantly, we try to look after every person who walks through our door like they are walking into our home."

She says the hospitality scene in Melbourne is all about community. "Some of the world's best modern cocktails have come out of this city, and so many of the world's best bars have roots tracing back to these local streets." She adds, "Melbourne is truly one of a kind, a cocktail with the best bits of Europe, the United Kingdom, and the United States. Others shine, but Melbourne will always be a heavyweight of hospitality."

CHANDELIER

BLACK PEARL
304 BRUNSWICK STREET, FITZROY

Melbourne is a beautiful mash of traditional and modern, with old-school architecture and a multitude of traditional cultures, as well as modern art, cutting-edge music, and locals with a taste for quality," Black Pearl director Tash Conte says. "This cocktail uses old-school ingredients with modern techniques to make a cocktail that is truly Melbourne." The Chandelier—a Sour—requires a short, hard shake, good quality ice, and the coldest glass you can get your hands on.

GLASSWARE: Coupe glass

GARNISH: Orange coin

- 1 oz. | 30 ml Never Never Triple Juniper Gin
- ⅔ oz. | 20 ml fresh lemon juice
- ½ oz. | 15 ml pineapple syrup
- ⅓ oz. | 10 ml Tio Pepe Fino Sherry
- ⅓ oz. | 10 ml Cocchi Americano
- 1 teaspoon | 5 ml grapefruit juice
- 4 dashes absinthe

1. Freeze a coupe glass. Combine all of the ingredients in a cocktail shaker with ice and shake.
2. Double-strain the cocktail into the frozen coupe and garnish with an orange coin.

APHRODITE'S ELIXIR OF DESIRE

Beverage and culture manager Max Wallace says Aphrodite's Elixir of Desire contains two major contributors to a love potion: passion and chocolate. "Add some tropical assistance via the passion fruit with pineapple and you have a seriously tasty crowd-pleaser," he says. "It's a taste of a holiday [vacation] at home."

GLASSWARE: Coupe glass

GARNISH: Passion fruit slice, shaved white chocolate

- 1½ oz. | 45 ml Baxter Australian Crafted Vodka
- 17/20 oz. | 25 ml Aubrey Passionfruit Liqueur
- ½ oz. | 15 ml white chocolate
- 17/20 oz. | 25 ml pineapple juice
- ⅓ oz. | 10 ml fresh lime juice

1. Chill a coupe glass. Combine all of the ingredients in a cocktail shaker with ice and shake for 30 seconds.
2. Double-strain the cocktail into the chilled coupe.
3. Garnish with a passion fruit slice and white chocolate shavings.

PRESTON CRACK

TAKEAWAY PIZZA
535 HIGH STREET, PRESTON

Venue manager Lauren Emmett says Takeaway Pizza's cocktails have a strong tropical focus all year round. "Who says you can't drink a Piña Colada in winter?" she asks. Preston Crack is a tongue-in-cheek name for the cocktail. "It gives a bit of a nod to it not only being so delicious it's addictive, but also the shady reputation Preston used to have way back when," she explains. "As devout Preston residents, we always have a chuckle with our customers when it's ordered." She advises using the original sriracha by Huy Fong Foods, as other sriracha brands have a very savory and meaty taste that doesn't hold up in this zesty, peachy drink.

GLASSWARE: Coupe glass

GARNISH: Dehydrated lime wheel

- **Sweet & Salty Mix (see recipe), for the rim**
- **1⅓ oz. | 40 ml Rooster Rojo Blanco Tequila**
- **1 oz. | 30 ml fresh lime juice**
- **½ oz. | 15 ml G.E. Massenez Crème de Pêche**

- **⅓ oz. | 10 ml Pierre Ferrand Dry Curaçao**
- **2 dashes The Bitter Truth Peach Bitters**
- **Squirt of sriracha**
- **Pinch red pepper flakes**

1. Chill a coupe glass. Dip the rim of the glass in water then into the Sweet & Salty Mix to give it a rim.
2. Combine all of the ingredients in a cocktail shaker with ice and give it a good hard shake for 10 seconds
3. Double-strain the cocktail into the chilled coupe.
4. Garnish with a dehydrated lime wheel.

SWEET & SALTY MIX: Mix together 50 grams Tajín, 50 grams Maldon Sea Salt Flakes, and 50 grams superfine (caster) sugar well, then store the mix in a container at room temperature.

SALTED GRAPEFRUIT PALOMA

THE KEYS LEISURE CENTRE
1/188 PLENTY ROAD, PRESTON

The Keys is an all-in-one leisure center and reimagined vintage bowling alley, with a sprawling beer garden, lanes, arcade, bar, and bistro. "This isn't the bowling alley from your tenth birthday party though," says bartender Morgan Cook. The Salted Grapefruit Paloma is "an easy drinking banger! Tangy, salty, and encapsulating fun," Cook says. One of the cocktail's hero ingredients is RHUBI Mistelle, an Australian rhubarb-based aperitif that adds a unique flavor and color to the drink. Meanwhile, the soda is made with natural mineral water just down the road in Macedon.

GLASSWARE: Highball glass
GARNISH: 2 dashes Tabasco sauce (optional), lime wedge

- Tajín, for the rim
- 1⅓ oz. | 40 ml añejo tequila
- ⅔ oz. | 20 ml RHUBI Mistelle
- ⅔ oz. | 20 ml fresh lime juice
- Strangelove Salted Grapefruit Soda, to top

1. Wet the rim of a highball glass then dip the glass in Tajín to give it a rim.
2. Combine the tequila, RHUBI Mistelle, and lime juice in a cocktail shaker with ice and shake very hard.
3. Pour the cocktail into the rimmed highball.
4. Top with the soda and, if using, garnish with 2 dashes Tabasco sauce and a lime wedge.

LA MAISON PIÑA

BAR MARGAUX
BASEMENT/111 LONSDALE STREET

Venue manager Nat Yao describes Bar Margaux as "coquettish and cosmopolitan," a place where "visitors are enticed to sink into our crimson leather booths for Martinis and oysters until the early hours," she says. La Maison Piña has all the delights of a Piña Colada with a touch of French flair. "Be sure to shake this one hard," Yao says. "If you have a big block of ice, it's ideal to ensure everything mixes well with the coconut cream."

GLASSWARE: Goblet

GARNISH: Pineapple leaves, cherries

- 1½ oz. | 45 ml pineapple juice
- 1 oz. | 30 ml aged rum
- 1 oz. | 30 ml cognac
- ¾ oz. | 22.5 ml Coco López Cream of Coconut
- 1 teaspoon | 5 ml fresh lime juice
- 3 dashes absinthe

1. Combine all of the ingredients in a cocktail shaker with ice and shake.
2. Strain the cocktail into a goblet with crushed ice.
3. Garnish with pineapple leaves and cherries.

CUMQUAT + WHITE TEA KOMBUCHA (NA)

MOLLI
20 MOLLISON STREET, ABBOTSFORD

Molli is a neighbourhood bar and bistro that fosters community connections with its familiar and approachable vibe, while embracing sustainability and seasonality in its menu. Bar manager Kayla Saito says kombucha is one of those "treat bevvies" that can be enjoyed while not having alcohol. "It's fermented, meaning tons of healthy gut bacteria and incredibly low ABV," she says. "It's a perfect delicious serve for the neighborhood, with a cult following since COVID-19." This recipe is for a batch preparation.

GLASSWARE: Wineglass
GARNISH: Fresh cumquat

- **51 oz. | 1,450 ml Kombucha Tea (see recipe)**
- **13½ oz. | 400 ml water**
- **5 oz. | 150 ml cumquat syrup**

1. Chill a wineglass. Combine all of the ingredients in a large container and chill it in the refrigerator.
2. To serve, pour the bubbly batch over ice into the chilled wine glass.
3. Garnish with a cumquat.

KOMBUCHA TEA: Boil 34 oz. (1 liter) water, steep 1 oz. (2 bags) tea for 15 minutes, strain, and add 10 oz. (300 ml) cold water and 60 grams raw sugar. Stir to combine and let the sweet tea batch cool. Rinse the SCOBY and add it along with 2 oz. (60 ml) kombucha starter (backslop). Store the kombucha tea in a kombucha jar with a cloth over the top. Ferment the tea at room temperature for 2 to 5 days depending on how acidic you'd like the batch.

GOLDEN GAYTIME

LILAC WINE BAR
31 STEPHENSON STREET, CREMORNE

Bar manager Kayla Saito says the inspiration for the Golden Gaytime came from asking Lilac's chefs what they loved to eat as a nostalgic treat, something they would choose to indulge in at that very moment that was also iconic to Australia. "It was hot in the kitchen as per usual, with the large wood-fired oven, and they immediately came up with a Golden Gaytime," Saito recalls. The Golden Gaytime is a beloved Australian frozen ice cream on a stick that features toffee-and-vanilla-flavored ice cream dipped in a chocolate coating and covered in biscuit pieces. "This cocktail is so popular and impressionable with our guests because of the nostalgia behind the flavor. Everyone gets it right away," she says. This Milk Punch recipe produces a batch of 3 cups (750 ml) so you'll have enough for a party when the time is right.

GLASSWARE: Rocks glass

GARNISH: Salted chocolate malt biscuit

- 13½ oz. | 400 ml whole milk
- 3½ oz. | 100 ml caramel
- 2½ oz. | 75 ml melted anglaise/ice cream
- 2½ oz. | 75 ml vanilla syrup
- ½ oz. | 15 ml saline solution
- 2 teaspoons | 8 grams malt powder
- 8 oz. | 250 ml Starward Two-Fold Whisky
- 1¾ oz. | 50 ml amontillado sherry
- ⅔ oz. | 20 ml lactic acid solution

1. Combine the milk, caramel, ice cream, syrup, saline solution, and malt powder in a large container and gently stir.

2. Pour in the whiskey, sherry, and lactic acid solution and gently stir. Then leave the mixture overnight in the refrigerator so the proteins separate out and the milk curdles.

3. Strain the mixture through a coffee filter and repeat as necessary until it runs clear. Bottle the punch.

4. To serve, measure out 2½ oz. (75 ml) per cocktail and pour it over a large rock of ice.

5. Garnish with a salted chocolate malt biscuit.

MELON ME MAYBE

DESSOUS
BASEMENT/164 FLINDERS LANE

Dessous bar manager Sandra Elizabeth says everyone in Melbourne loves a good basement bar. "And Dessous is exactly that! *Dessous* means 'basement' in French, and when you come down the stairs, you'll immediately fall in love with the dark, cozy interior and dimly lit backbar," she says. The Melon Me Maybe is fruity without being too sweet, yet refreshing and completely smashable. "The light vegetal flavors of the cucumber marry with the gentle sweetness of the Lillet Blanc, giving the cocktail the herbaceous notes it needs to cut through the sweetness of the melon and yuzu. Throw in Australia's favorite gin brand—Four Pillars—as the base spirit, and you've got a best seller!" Elizabeth's "inspiration behind the drink was to do a riff of a Bamboo, but I decided to swap out sherry for the melon aperitif to cater to the customers of Dessous, who lean toward fruity, refreshing cocktails." You'll need a carbonation rig and pressure-proof bottles for this recipe.

GLASSWARE: Highball glass

GARNISH: Cucumber ribbon, lemon wedge

- 2⅔ oz. | 80 ml Capi Yuzu Soda

- 1 oz. | 30 ml melon aperitif

- ⅔ oz. | 20 ml Cucumber Rapid-Infused Lillet Blanc (see recipe)

- ½ oz. | 15 ml Four Pillars Yuzu Gin

- 2½ teaspoons | 12 ml verjus

- 5 dashes | 3 ml simple syrup

- Saline solution, to taste

1. Combine all of the ingredients in a measuring vessel.
2. Pour the mixture into pressure-proof bottles, filling them halfway.
3. Force carbonate the bottles 3 times at 50 psi.
4. Chill the mixture in the refrigerator.
5. Line the inside of a highball glass with cucumber ribbons.
6. Add ice cubes, then gently pour the carbonated cocktail into the glass.
7. Garnish with a lemon wedge and serve with a straw.

CUCUMBER RAPID-INFUSED LILLET BLANC: Peel 1 Lebanese cucumber and cut it into thin half slices. Combine the cucumber slices and 16 oz. (500 ml) Lillet Blanc in an iSi cream whipper. Use 4 cream chargers, briefly shaking after each charge. After the final charge, let the cream whipper sit for 30 minutes. Strain the mixture and bottle it.

FULL AUTONOMY

Bar manager Dhanyia Passcuran describes Dom's as a "three-level wonderland. Each level of the venue holds a unique experience. Level one is our pizzeria for hosting dinner parties or dates; level two is our pool room; and level three is our outdoor rooftop bar with a delightful view down Swanston Street." Full Autonomy showcases a local producer—Autonomy Distillers, which is located just down the road from the bar in Spotswood. Davo Plum Aperitivo Bitters balances tart Davidson plum, a sour native Australian plum grown in tropical rainforests, and rosella flowers with sweet Australian oranges and a hint of Tasmanian pepperberry. It is sweet with a hint of bitterness—expect flavors of plum, citrus, and raspberry with a slight peppery finish. "Just make sure to give the drink a vigorous shake on ice to amp up that smooth foam," Passcuran advises.

GLASSWARE: Rocks glass

GARNISH: Dried citrus

- 1 oz. | 30 ml Autonomy Davo Plum Aperitivo Bitters
- 1 oz. | 30 ml Autonomy Native Australian Amaro
- 1 oz. | 30 ml fresh lemon juice
- ⅓ oz. | 10 ml simple syrup
- Wonderfoam Cocktail Foamer, as needed

1. Combine all of the ingredients in a cocktail shaker and dry-shake (without ice) to activate the Wonderfoam.

2. Add ice and shake vigorously.

3. Double-strain the cocktail into a rocks glass with fresh ice.

4. Garnish with dried citrus.

GAME OF ZEN

1806

169 EXHIBITION STREET

Step through the doors of 1806 and you are transported to the Prohibition era. "We always have conversations with the guests," bartender Marcus Cooper says, "and when they ask for a recommendation, it's a journey that we want to take with them. We know how special it feels to discover something new and exciting, so we always try to give every guest the same experience. And if they want the usual, we're there to give them that comfort too." The Game of Zen is an ode to Melbourne's most famous cocktail creation, the Japanese Slipper. "It promises something different to most palates, but the ingredients read as welcoming, familiar even," he explains. "Kombu can be forgiving since it releases a lot of flavor in a short amount of time, but you'll want to dehydrate the cucumber so the tequila isn't watered down and retains its bite," he says. The recipes for 1806's Cucumber-Infused Tequila and Kombu Seaweed–Infused Shochu are closely guarded secrets, but here are some simple approximations for you to mix at home.

GLASSWARE: Nick & Nora glass

- 1⅓ oz. | 40 ml Cucumber-Infused Tequila (see recipe)
- ⅔ oz. | 20 ml Kombu Seaweed–Infused Shochu (see recipe)
- ⅔ oz. | 20 ml verjus
- ½ oz. | 15 ml Giffard Matcha Green Tea Syrup

1. Combine all of the ingredients in a cocktail shaker with ice and shake.

2. Fine-strain the cocktail into a Nick & Nora.

CUCUMBER-INFUSED TEQUILA: Wash 1 cucumber and chop it into chunks, then place the cucumber chunks in a clean, airtight container and pour 1 (750 ml) bottler of tequila over them. Seal the container and let the mixture infuse at room temperature for 24 to 48 hours. Strain and rebottle the infused tequila.

KOMBU SEAWEED–INFUSED SHOCHU: Add 15 grams kombu to a sterilized jar then pour 1 (750 ml) bottle of shochu into the jar. Seal the container and allow the mixture to infuse overnight. Strain and rebottle the infused shochu.

THE DEVIL WAS AN ANGEL

Mesa Verde melds traditional Mexican flavors with Australian ones. "We are one of the premier mezcal and tequila bars in the country," says bar supervisor Mima Whitewolf, "and each personality behind our bar is forever chomping at the bit to find the perfect drop for our clientele." The Devil Was an Angel is a take on the traditional Toreador updated for Melbourne's modern, well-travelled, and particularly epicurean palate. "People here want punchy," Whitewolf says. The mezcal "shines through and complements the tart apricot and deep hickory to produce a cocktail that is at once sultry and smashable."

GLASSWARE: Nick & Nora glass

GARNISH: Angostura bitters hearts

- 1 oz. | 30 ml Mezcal Derrumbes Oaxaca

- 1 oz. | 30 ml G.E. Massenez Liqueur d'Abricot

- ⅔ oz. | 20 ml fresh lime juice

- 1 teaspoon | 5 ml light agave nectar

- 2 drops Mister Bitters Honeyed Apricot & Smoked Hickory Bitters

- 1 egg white

1. Combine all of the ingredients in a Boston shaker without ice and dry-shake as hard as possible to froth the egg white.
2. Add ice and shake again.
3. Double-strain the cocktail into a Nick & Nora.
4. Garnish with Angostura bitters in the shape of 3 hearts.

SHIRAZ GIN FIZZ

DEXTER
456 HIGH STREET, PRESTON

Dexter aims to bring a city vibe to Preston, a suburb located northeast of Melbourne's central business district. "Dexter seasonally changes its cocktail menu, but every time I went to take the Shiraz Gin Fizz off the menu, customers would ask for it," bar manager Emma Hull says. "So it is very much a staple here now!"

GLASSWARE: Highball glass

GARNISH: Dehydrated orange wedge

- 1⅓ oz. | 40 ml Four Pillars Bloody Shiraz Gin
- ½ oz. | 15 ml Lemon Myrtle Cordial (see recipe)

- Capi Yuzu Soda, to top
- Capi Soda, to top

1. Combine the gin and cordial in a highball and fill the glass to the top with ice.

2. Top with half yuzu soda and half soda and give the drink a good stir with a barspoon.

3. Garnish with a dehydrated orange wedge.

LEMON MYRTLE CORDIAL: In a saucepan over medium-high heat, combine 2 cups water, 1 cup superfine (caster) sugar, the juice of 4 lemons, and the zest of 1 to 2 lemons and bring the mixture to a simmer, stirring until the sugar is dissolved. Remove the pan from heat, add ¾ cup fresh myrtle leaves, washed, and allow the cordial to steep for at least 30 minutes. Strain and store the cordial in the refrigerator.

GINGER MARGARITA

LOBBY LOUNGE
THE WESTIN MELBOURNE, GROUND FLOOR,
205 COLLINS STREET

L ocated in the heart of Melbourne's theatre district, The Westin offers sophisticated yet relaxed surroundings. Food and beverage manager Eloise Kerr says there are three reasons why the Ginger Margarita is a favorite with customers: guests love a twist on a classic, Melburnians love tequila, and the recipe provides spice in a more mellow way than chile peppers.

GLASSWARE: Rocks glass

GARNISH: Candied ginger

- Salt, for the rim
- 1½ oz. | 45 ml tequila
- 1 oz. | 30 ml Cointreau
- 1 oz. | 30 ml fresh lime juice
- ¾ oz. | 20 ml ginger syrup

1. Wet the rim of a rocks glass then dip the rim in salt. Combine the remaining ingredients in a cocktail shaker with ice and shake.

2. Strain the cocktail into the rimmed glass.

3. Garnish with candied ginger.

NO ONE MOURNS THE WICKED

LOBBY LOUNGE
THE WESTIN MELBOURNE, GROUND FLOOR,
205 COLLINS STREET

During the Melbourne season of the musical phenomenon *Wicked*, Westin Melbourne created a series of cocktails inspired by the production, including No One Mourns the Wicked, which features a bewitching mix of Black Galliano, Chambord, and Cointreau. "It's dramatic and is an uncommon blend," food and beverage manager Eloise Kerr says. "The results are theatrical and broody." She adds, "Don't over-spritz it with the soda! The stretch should make it refreshing and open up the orange citrus notes in the drink. We prefer to serve the cocktail in a purple-tinted glass to intensify the dramatic inky coloring."

GLASSWARE: Purple wineglass
GARNISH: Black licorice ribbon

- ½ oz. | 15 ml Cointreau
- ½ oz. | 15 ml Chambord
- ½ oz. | 15 ml raspberry balsamic vinegar
- 17/20 oz. | 25 ml Galliano Sambuca Black
- Soda water, to top

1. Combine all of the ingredients, except for the soda, in a cocktail shaker with ice and shake.
2. Strain the cocktail into a glass filled halfway with ice.
3. Top with soda water.
4. Garnish with a black licorice ribbon.

THE PEAR-CILLIN

SIGLO BAR
2/161 SPRING STREET

Siglo, established in 2007, is a stunning cube of industrial steel, glass, and neon opening to striking city views spanning the flood-lit columned facade of Parliament, the spire of St Patrick's Cathedral, and the mural-covered brickwork and domes of the Princess Theatre. It is also home to one of the few remaining cigar bars in town. Mel-burnians and their friends come to soak in the cocktails, cigars, and culture. The original Penicillin was created by Melbourne-born bar-tender Sam Ross while living in New York in the mid-2000s and work-ing at Milk & Honey. Siglo's take gives this whiskey-based drink an even sweeter twist with the addition of fruit and a flashy garnish. "The flour-ishing pear garnish on the Pear-cillin entices patrons every single time and hints at the sweet fruity flavor ahead," Krishaal Kumaran says.

GLASSWARE: Rocks glass

GARNISH: Pear fan

- 1½ oz. | 45 ml Glenfiddich
- ½ oz. | 15 ml Johnnie Walker Black Label
- ½ oz. | 15 ml G.E. Massenez Eau de Vie Poire Williams
- ½ oz. | 15 ml cinnamon-infused honey syrup (2:1)
- 2 drops saline solution

1. Combine the two whiskies and the liqueur in a mixing glass and stir.
2. Add the spirits mixture to a cocktail shaker with the remaining in-gredients and ice and shake until well chilled.
3. Double-strain the cocktail into a rocks glass over a large ice rock.
4. Garnish with a pear fan.

LYNDEN BARNES, LITTLE LON DISTILLING CO.

Located in the last remaining single-story cottage in Melbourne's central business district, the bar at Little Lon Distilling Co. oozes charm and history. "It was built in 1877 and all of the spirits we make tell the story of its prior inhabitants—mostly centered around its place in history as Melbourne's former red-light district," venue manager Lynden Barnes explains.

Today, the three-room cottage is licensed to host twenty people in its bar, with a gin still housed in one room and fermentation tanks in the other.

The gins Barnes pours take inspiration from the area's notorious past. The Ginger Mick, for example, is named after Australian author and poet C.J. Dennis's book character Ginger Mick.

In 1915, Dennis famously described the Little Lon district as being favored by "low, degraded broots" (brutes).

"We embrace the questionable histories of Little Lon and enjoy keeping the stories alive," says Barnes.

GINTARITO

LITTLE LON DISTILLING CO
17 CASSELDEN PLACE

Venue manager Lynden Barnes says the Gintarito is very refreshing, easy to make, and has the perfect mix of sweet and sour. "It's hard to stop at one of these when the sun is out," he says. He adds that it wouldn't "be out of place slurped on a sunny day at the beach in St Kilda". He advises the distillery's Ginger Mick Gin is perfect in this cocktail. "Use other gins at your own risk," he jokes. "Also, it *must* be made with fresh juices, and always use a good quality grapefruit soda."

GLASSWARE: Highball glass

GARNISH: Dehydrated orange slice

- 1½ oz. | 45 ml Little Lon Ginger Mick Gin
- ½ oz. | 15 ml fresh orange juice
- ½ oz. | 15 ml fresh lime juice
- ½ oz. | 15 ml fresh lemon juice
- ½ oz. | 15 ml Vanilla Bean Simple Syrup (see recipe)
- Grapefruit soda, to top

1. Fill a highball glass with ice.
2. Add all of the ingredients, except for the soda, to the glass and lightly stir.
3. Top with grapefruit soda and garnish with a dehydrated orange slice.

VANILLA BEAN SIMPLE SYRUP: In a small saucepan over medium-low heat, combine 1 cup water and 1 cup sugar and simmer, stirring, until the sugar is dissolved. Slice a vanilla bean in half lengthwise and add the bean halves to the simple syrup, stirring. Remove the syrup from heat, let it cool, and strain.

SALTED GRAPEFRUIT

BY STRANGELOVE

180mL

CLOUDY DELIGHT

MORTIMER'S BAR
PULLMAN MELBOURNE ALBERT PARK,
65 QUEENS ROAD, ALBERT PARK

Mortimer's Bar takes its name from the hotel group's founder, George Mortimer Pullman. It is known for its relaxed atmosphere and gin cocktails, offering a modern take on a gin bar with a nod to the glamour and service of old-school hotels. The Cloudy Delight is "a sophisticated cocktail and with a beautiful purple color. It's as visually pleasing as it is unique and delicious," food and beverage duty manager Kim Cuong (Jay) Hoang says. "The Cloudy Delight was inspired by the view of Albert Park Lake and Melbourne CBD from the hotel when the semi-clouded sky is painted with a beautiful purple and pinkish color at sunset."

GLASSWARE: Wineglass

GARNISH: Dehydrated orange wheel, fairy floss, sprig of rosemary

- 1 oz. | 30 ml Mortimer Gin
- ⅔ oz. | 20 ml Chambord
- ½ oz. | 15 ml Vok Parfait Amour Liqueur
- ⅓ oz. | 10 ml simple syrup
- ⅓ oz. | 10 ml aquafaba
- 1½ oz. | 45 ml lemon squash or lemon soda
- 1½ oz. | 45 ml tonic water

1. Combine all of the ingredients, except for the lemon squash/ soda and tonic, in a cocktail shaker without ice and dry-shake.

2. Add ice and shake well again.

3. Add ice, the lemon squash, and the tonic to a wineglass.

4. Strain the cocktail from the shaker into the glass.

5. Garnish with a dehydrated orange wheel, fairy floss, and sprig of rosemary.

IRISH COFFEE

ANTIQUE BAR
218 GLENHUNTLY ROAD, ELSTERNWICK

Antique Bar owner Boutaina Richardson says the bar's Irish Coffee has been a hit to date, as patrons love the mix of coffee and whiskey. "Before putting it on our menu we tried various coffee roasters and were lucky to come across Omar & The Marvellous Coffee Bird just two kilometers away from the bar," she explains. "We tried three different whiskies with two coffee blends and with a unanimous vote settled for the white blend and Powers Gold Label Whiskey. There's something about the cold cream contrasting Omar's coffee that wins over customers. The cocktail is smooth, easy to drink, and prefect for all year round, as we make an iced version in the warmer months."

GLASSWARE: Irish coffee mug or glass
GARNISH: Fresh cream

- **3 oz. | 90 ml Omar & the Marvellous Coffee Bird White Blend**
- **1 oz. | 30 ml Powers Gold Label Irish Whiskey**
- **½ oz. | 15 ml simple syrup**

1. Warm a coffee mug. Combine all of the ingredients in the heated mug and stir.
2. Garnish with cold fresh cream.

COFFEE HOUSE

HEARTBREAKER
234A RUSSELL STREET

Assistant venue manager Blue Valentine says Heartbreaker is more than just a bar. "It's a feeling. The music is loud, the drinks are cold, and the vibes are high," she says. "It's a good-time, American-style bar, serving great booze, pool, and New York–style pizza by the slice to the sounds of a retro jukebox into the early hours. Everything about the bar is emotional, and that's what people fall in love with. We are known for a great selection of craft beer across our rotating taps, and a backbar full of American whiskey, tequila, and mezcal."

GLASSWARE: Rocks glass

GARNISH: Lemon twist

- 1½ oz. | 45 ml tequila
- ¾ oz. | 22 ml coffee liqueur
- 2 dashes orange bitters

1. In the order of ingredients listed, build the cocktail in a rocks glass with ice.

2. Garnish with a lemon twist.

THE EVERLEIGH
BOTTLING Cº

COFFEE
HOUSE

MANUFACTURED TO THE
MOST EXACTING STANDARDS
UPSTAIRS 150 GERTRUDE STR
. FITZROY, VICTORIA 3065

GUY MIRON, GINNY'S LOUNGE

Melbourne is known as an innovative mecca for food and drinks, something bar manager Guy Miron aims to reflect in the cocktail list at Ginny's Lounge.

"As the flagship bar of Brunswick Aces, Australia's first nonalcoholic distillery, we pride ourselves on being an inclusive space where everyone is welcome, regardless of their preference or ability to consume alcoholic beverages," says Miron.

"Our unique offering of high-quality nonalcoholic spirits and a menu that offers both nonalcoholic and alcoholic on all the beverages options is what sets us apart in the hospitality scene, ensuring that all our guests can enjoy a sophisticated drink experience.

"Customers also love the ambience at our bar. We blend Victorian chic with a laid-back Melbourne style, creating a cozy and inviting atmosphere perfect for any season."

WELLNESS

Bar manager Guy Miron says the health-conscious nature of Melburnians is mirrored in Ginny's Wellness cocktail, which uses fresh, high-quality ingredients. "Melbourne's often chilly and wintry weather is countered by the comforting, warming flavors of our cocktail," he says. "Everyone is trying their best to do good to their body and we are here to help with that. As this drink is not high on sugar and has a healthy dose of apple cider vinegar, they experience exactly that. No wonder that the second name for this cocktail is 'I Gut You.'" Miron advises discarding the tea bags immediately after you finish boiling them, as the tannins can create an unpleasant bitterness. To include everyone, you can use both alcoholic and nonalcoholic gin options for the drink.

GLASSWARE: Rocks glass

GARNISH: Cinnamon powder

- 1½ oz. | 45 ml fresh apple juice
- 1 oz. | 30 ml Brunswick Aces Hearts Gin or Brunswick Acies Sapiir (Non-Alcoholic Gin)
- ⅔ oz. | 20 ml Earl Grey Syrup (see recipe)
- ⅔ oz. | 20 ml apple cider vinegar
- ½ oz. | 15 ml egg white or 5 drops Wonderfoam Cocktail Foamer

shaker and dry-shake (without ice).

2. Add ice and shake again.

3. Pour the cocktail into a rocks glass filled halfway with ice.

4. With a card or a paper cover half of the glass and sprinkle the drink lightly with cinnamon powder. Remove the card. If you want to unleash your inner artist, use a toothpick as a paintbrush and style a design.

EARL GREY SYRUP: Preheat 8 oz. (250 ml) water in a kettle then pour it into a metal saucepan over high heat. Boil the water with 3 bags of Earl Grey tea for 5 minutes. Remove from heat, remove the tea bags and discard them, and add 200 grams sugar. Whisk until the sugar is completely dissolved. Allow the syrup to cool, pour it into a bottle, and label it.

THE DAN MURPHIZZ

DAN'S DINER
FEDERATION SQUARE

Daniel Francis Murphy, a third-generation winemaker, opened his first store in Prahran in 1952, which you can still visit at 282 Chapel Street. Rather than being something that was reserved for the wealthy and elite, Dan's vision was to democratize wine and make it easily accessible to everyone. Dan Murphy's now has more than 200 stores across Australia. During Melbourne Food and Wine Festival, Dan Murphy's brought a nostalgic 1950s-style diner experience to Federation Square. The food and drink menus were created by some of Melbourne's most well-regarded Dans since Daniel Francis Murphy himself. They included all-star chefs Dan Hunter (from Birregurra's three-hatted restaurant Brae) and Daniel Wilson (from fire-focused Japanese eatery Yakimono), while cocktail king Dan Docherty (co-owner and bartender at Commis) was the mastermind behind the drinks list.

GLASSWARE: Highball glass

GARNISH: Dehydrated lemon wheel, maraschino cherry on a skewer

- 1 oz. | 30 ml MGC Melbourne Dry Gin
- ⅔ oz. | 20 ml Marionette Apricot Brandy
- ⅔ oz. | 20 ml fresh lemon juice
- ⅔ oz. | 20 ml simple syrup
- Dash Wonderfoam Cocktail Foamer
- 3½ oz. | 100 ml soda water

1. Combine all of the ingredients, except for the soda, in a cocktail shaker with ice and shake vigorously.
2. Pour the soda water into a highball.
3. Strain the cocktail over the soda and top with ice to fill the glass.
4. Garnish with a dehydrated lemon wheel and a maraschino cherry on a skewer.

DANHATTAN

A Melbourne twist on a classic Manhattan featuring a Melburnian whiskey stirred down with Maidenii Sweet Vermouth, macadamia liqueur, and bitters. Take that, New York.

GLASSWARE: Coupe or rocks glass

GARNISH: Orange twist

- 1½ oz. | 45 ml Starward Two-Fold Whisky
- 17/20 oz. | 25 ml Maidenii Sweet Vermouth
- ⅔ oz. | 20 ml Mac. Liqueur by Brookie's
- Dash Angostura bitters

1. Combine all of the ingredients in a mixing glass filled with ice.
2. Stir down thoroughly with a barspoon for approximately 30 seconds to allow the ice to dilute and chill the spirits.
3. Strain the cocktail into a chilled coupe glass or alternatively a rocks glass with an oversized ice cube.
4. Garnish with an orange twist.

LIBERTY OLD FASHIONED

BAR LIBERTY
234 JOHNSTON STREET, FITZROY

Bar Liberty prides itself on having an offering that revolves around smaller producers "creating interesting things made with passion and intrigue," says bar manager Ludovic Beauchamp-Chatel. "The Liberty Old Fashioned highlights local fortified producer Pennyweight, ensuring it's something unique to the venue. The idea that less is more when it comes to building a cocktail ensures the quality local ingredients are identifiable in the drink, which makes it shine. He recommends serving "the cocktail from the freezer. This enhances viscosity and texture and ensures consistency."

GLASSWARE: Rocks glass

GARNISH: Honeycomb

- **2 oz. | 60 ml Starward HER Honeycomb**

- **1 teaspoon | 5 ml Pennyweight Muscat**
- **Orange bitters, to taste**

1. In the order of ingredients listed, build the cocktail in a rocks glass.

2. Stir the ingredients down and serve them on an ice rock.

3. Garnish with honeycomb.

NICK TESAR, FOUR PILLARS

Nick Tesar is creative director of gin drinks at Four Pillars. Formerly bar manager at Bar Liberty in Fitzroy, he has won multiple bartender awards including Diageo World Class Australian Bartender of the Year 2022.

Nick went on to compete against the world's best in the World Class global finals, where he took the runner-up accolade. He joined Four Pillars in May 2023, with the team describing him as "one of the real modern drinks masters of Australia."

"I have watched the Four Pillars story from its very beginning—I was in fact bartending at Gin Palace in 2013 when they had their actual launch—so it has been some sort of coming full circle," says Nick.

When it comes to the Melbourne bar scene's love for gin and Four Pillars, Nick explains: "It's our backyard. We have such great and often personal relationships with so many of the bars and bartenders in the community. We feel like they tell our story and represent the product incredibly well in the drinks they serve and the stories they share. And in doing so, they get to celebrate the local product, which is always a point of pride.

"Melbourne has always excelled in telling a passionate story of what's around it. Whether spirits, wine, beer, ingredients, whatever it may be, staff get genuinely excited to show off something new, different, or that they feel a connection with."

BLOODY SHIRAZ SOUR

FOUR PILLARS
2A LILYDALE ROAD, HEALESVILLE

Four Pillars is an hour's drive from Melbourne, but it is closely connected to its heart. Established in 2013 in the Yarra Valley, it has become Australia's number one craft spirit. The Bloody Shiraz Sour has cult status at the distillery, and while no longer on the menu, it is always available. "This is my take on it, showcasing a distillery classic, blended with a modern classic cocktail, that has served me well through years of bartending," creative director Nick Tesar says. "It is stunning in appearance, has a great texture, but most importantly the lemon and Bloody Shiraz Gin combination is bloody delicious. Such an easy sip that works all year round." When making the cocktail, Tesar suggests combining all the ingredients in a tin but adding only one ice cube to start with and shake. "This will whip all the ingredients up while combining them with the egg white," he says.

GLASSWARE: Rocks glass

- 1¾ oz. | 50 ml Four Pillars Bloody Shiraz Gin
- 17/20 oz. | 25 ml fresh lemon juice
- ⅔ oz. | 20 ml egg white
- ⅓ oz. | 10 ml Marionette Mûre
- 1 teaspoon | 5 ml simple syrup

1. Combine all of the ingredients in a cocktail shaker and shake once without ice and again with ice.

2. Strain the cocktail into a rocks glass.

MEASUREMENT CONVERSIONS

	1 dash		0.625 ml
	4 dashes		2.5 ml
	1 teaspoon		5 ml
¼ oz.			7.5 ml
⅓ oz.	2 teaspoons		10 ml
½ oz.	3 teaspoons	1 tablespoon	15 ml
⅔ oz.	4 teaspoons		20 ml
¾ oz.			22.5 ml
17/20 oz.			25 ml
1 oz.		2 tablespoons	30 ml
1 ½ oz.		3 tablespoons	45 ml
1 ¾ oz.			52.5 ml
2 oz.	4 tablespoons	¼ cup	60 ml
8 oz.		1 cup	250 ml
16 oz.	1 pint	2 cups	500 ml
24 oz.		3 cups	750 ml
32 oz.	1 quart	4 cups	1 liter (1,000 ml)

ACKNOWLEDGMENTS

Thank you to the bar managers, bartenders, and owners who generously contributed their recipes and photos to this book.

Cheers to all the wonderful friends who clink glasses with me throughout the year as I explore new bars and old favorites through my drinks writing.

I will also be forever grateful to my partner, David Fuller, for his patience and support as I wrestled with hundreds of cocktail recipes, images, and interviews over many nights and weekends.

And thank you to the team at Cider Mill Press for their guidance and expertise, with a special shout out to Jeremy Hauck and Lindy Pokorny.

ABOUT THE AUTHOR

Alana House is the founder and editor of Drinks Digest, a website focused on drinks news and the Australian bar scene. She has been a drinks writer for more than ten years and was a judge at the 2024 Australian Gin Awards.

Prior to her career in drinks, Alana worked in women's lifestyle magazines, including *Australian Cosmopolitan* and Singapore *Harper's Bazaar*. She also edited magazines ranging from *Singapore CLEO* to *Everyday Food* and *Woman's Day*.

During her digital career Alana has been an editor and content creator at leading Australian news and lifestyle websites including Mamamia and Escape.

Discover more about Australian cocktails and the talented bartenders behind them at drinksdigest.com.

PHOTO CREDITS

Pages 13 Jack Lovel; 16–17, 24, 253, 255, 261 Jake Roden; 20–21 Carmen Zammit; 30–31 Kristoffer Paulsen; 35 Kim Jane Photography; 43 Ryan McCurdy; 44 Davey van Niftrik; 57 Bonnie Savage; 58 Nick Da Fonseca Photography; 62, 71 Arianna Harry Photography; 72 Ren Pidgeon; 73 Andrew Griffiths; 77 Mikey J White; 81 Griffin Simm; 87 Ferdi Photography; 96, 98, 232 Tash Sorensen; 97 Gareth Sobey Photography; 114 Samantha Schultz; 117 Graham Denholm; 138, 140 Hugh Davison; 144–145, 145, 147 Liana Hardy Photography; 153 David Griffen; 155 Harrison Moss; 161 Dean Schmideg; 185 Chip Mooney; 200, 203 Mark Chew; 208, 213 Jo McGann; 227 Ryal Sormaz; 257 David Li; 267, 268 by Ashley Ludkin; 275 Benito Martin Photography.

Pages 1, 3, 4–5, 9, 14–15, 23, 25 used under official license from Shutterstock.com.

Pages 8, 10 courtesy of State Library Victoria.

All other images courtesy of the respective bars, restaurants, and interviewees.

INDEX

—ABOUT CIDER MILL PRESS BOOK PUBLISHERS—

Good ideas ripen with time. From seed to harvest, Cider Mill Press brings fine reading, information, and entertainment together between the covers of its creatively crafted books. Our Cider Mill bears fruit twice a year, publishing a new crop of titles each spring and fall.

"Where Good Books Are Ready for Press"
501 Nelson Place
Nashville, Tennessee 37214
cidermillpress.com

— MAP OF —

— MELBOURNE AND SUBURBS —